Using Student Feedback for Successful Teaching

Feedback from students to teachers has been shown to have a major influence on students' achievement. Although the use of feedback from students requires little time and investment, the exploration of this topic in recent years has focused primarily on that from teacher-to-student or teacher-to-teacher. This innovative book examines the much-neglected feedback path from student to teacher and provides an empirically founded and practice-oriented step-by-step guide for teachers who want to get feedback on their own teaching.

Including a foreword by John Hattie, the authors shed light on the benefits, challenges, impact and academic discussion of student feedback. Topics include:

- an outline of the current state of research about feedback, including in the light of Visible Learning, and the essentials for translating this research into implementation in the classroom;
- the advantages of student-to-teacher feedback and how it is connected to good, effective teaching;
- the practicalities of putting student feedback into practice: finding the right questions to ask, professional discussion, and how to go about applying changes to your teaching;
- an exploration of combining digital technologies with the acquisition and evaluation of student feedback;
- the wider impact of feedback and how a "feedback culture" can transform not only individual teachers but also whole schools.

Using Student Feedback for Successful Teaching is an essential guide for experienced and newly-qualified teachers alike who are invested in their professional development and who strive to deliver the best quality teaching for their students.

Klaus Zierer is Professor of Education at the University of Augsburg, Germany, and Associate Research Fellow of the Economic and Social Research Council (ESRC)-funded Centre on Skills, Knowledge, and Organisational Performance (SKOPE) at the University of Oxford, UK.

Benedikt Wisniewski is a school psychologist, former teacher, and teacher trainer. As a lecturer at the University of Regensburg, he is involved in university teacher training. He is the author and publisher of various textbooks in the field of pedagogy and educational psychology.

Using Student Feedback for Successful Teaching

Klaus Zierer and
Benedikt Wisniewski

LONDON AND NEW YORK

First published 2019
by Routledge
2 Park Square, Milton Park, Abingdon, Oxon OX14 4RN

and by Routledge
711 Third Avenue, New York, NY 10017

Routledge is an imprint of the Taylor & Francis Group, an informa business

© 2019 Klaus Zierer and Benedikt Wisniewski

The right of Klaus Zierer and Benedikt Wisniewski to be identified as authors of this work has been asserted by them in accordance with sections 77 and 78 of the Copyright, Designs and Patents Act 1988.

All rights reserved. No part of this book may be reprinted or reproduced or utilised in any form or by any electronic, mechanical, or other means, now known or hereafter invented, including photocopying and recording, or in any information storage or retrieval system, without permission in writing from the publishers.

Trademark notice: Product or corporate names may be trademarks or registered trademarks, and are used only for identification and explanation without intent to infringe.

British Library Cataloguing-in-Publication Data
A catalogue record for this book is available from the British Library

Library of Congress Cataloging-in-Publication Data
A catalog record for this book has been requested

ISBN: 978-1-138-54579-3 (hbk)
ISBN: 978-1-138-54581-6 (pbk)
ISBN: 978-1-351-00196-0 (ebk)

Typeset in Bembo and Helvetica Neue
by Apex CoVantage, LLC

Contents

List of illustrations		*vi*
Acknowledgments		*ix*
Foreword by John Hattie		*x*
1	Introduction: feedback between desire and reality	1
2	Feedback in the light of Visible Learning	5
3	Student feedback	27
4	Student feedback in practice	37
5	Student feedback scenarios using digitization	80
6	Feedback culture and professionalism	95
	Index	*111*

Illustrations

Figures

2.1	Distribution of all effect sizes observed in Visible Learning	8
2.2	Effect size of the "class size" factor	9
2.3	Scientific research on feedback	10
2.4	Effect size of the "feedback" factor	12
2.5	Types of feedback in schools	13
2.6	Levels of feedback	14
2.7	Feedback on three levels	17
2.8	Feedback provider and feedback recipient	21
2.9	Feedback from teacher to learner	21
2.10	Feedback from learners to learners	21
2.11	Feedback from teachers to teachers	23
2.12	Feedback from learners to teachers	24
3.1	Johari window	29
3.2	Speaking time by teachers in the classroom – estimation and actual measurement	30
3.3	Didactic hexagon	34
4.1	Task example	39
4.2	Task example	39
4.3	Task example	40
4.4	Task example	41
4.5	Test result sheet	42
4.6	Feedback coordinate system	45
4.7	Feedback target	46
4.8	Feedback chart	47
4.9	Self-perception and student feedback	47
4.10	Steps to obtain feedback from lessons	50

4.11	Correlation between student feedback and achievement	53
4.12	Development of teaCh	58
4.13	Structural model of teaCh	60
4.14	Feedback on six items from the "Captivate" category	64
4.15	The process following feedback	67
4.16	Conditions for change	70
4.17	Levels of problems identified by student feedback	72
5.1	Four-step response option for questionnaire items	81
5.2	Feedback barometers	82
5.3	Comparison of perspectives	82
5.4	Response distribution	82
5.5	Results of the questionnaire on the classroom climate	84
5.6	Response distribution	85
5.7	Category barometers	87
5.8	Comparison of perspectives	88
5.9	Response distribution	88
5.10	Comparison of perspectives	90
5.11	Response distribution	91
5.12	Comparison of perspectives	93
6.1	System performance when introducing innovations	97
6.2	Innovation cycle	98
6.3	Competencies in the didactic triangle	105
6.4	Mindframes at the center of the didactic triangle	106
6.5	K3W Model	107

Tables

2.1	Most frequently studied factors	11
2.2	Percentage of different types of feedback in the classroom	16
2.3	Feedback matrix	20
3.1	Definitions of key concepts	33
4.1	Feedback methods overview	49
4.2	Types of questionnaires for classroom feedback	57
4.3	Criteria for successful feedback	63
4.4	Structured planning of a change process based on the SWOT analysis	71
4.5	Success-critical factors of change processes at the systemic level	75
5.1	Free-text annotations of students (selection)	91

Questionnaires

1	Classroom climate	83
2	Quality of teaching (extract from teaCh)	86
3	Items from the categories "Challenge" (extract from teaCh)	89
4	Control and Confer (extract from teaCh)	92
5	Feedback mindframes	100

Acknowledgments

We would like to thank Ingmar Bode, the CEO of FeedbackSchule, who gave us a lot of valuable suggestions thanks to his critical and constructive reading; Bruce Roberts, who joined us on the way to publishing our work for English-speaking countries; and Alice Gray, who patiently answered all our questions at Taylor & Francis. Our very special thanks go to John Hattie, who followed the development of this book with interest and always stood by our side with advice.

Foreword

The core message of Visible Learning is that teachers should see learning through the eyes of their students and that learners should be enabled to see themselves as their own teachers. With this statement, I try to emphasize how important it is for teachers to pay more attention to how their students learn. It is also important that students learn to solve problems instead of memorizing facts and data. Teachers are faced with the challenge of recognizing the impact they have on their students' learning experiences. For this purpose, it is necessary to shift the focus from monologue to dialogue and to bring learners from reactive listening to their own reflection – the latter especially in a collective way: talking together about what one knows or does not know, what one understands or does not understand, how ideas can be linked with other ideas, and how a transfer to new situations can be made. Enjoying the process of learning together is an important goal of school and teaching.

All these ideas are based on the power of feedback. Knowing one's own impact requires that one can use feedback to distinguish between effective and ineffective teaching. The self-assessment of teachers is not the decisive factor. Rather, it is the external information from learners that reveals the power of feedback in this context. In this respect, successful teachers demand feedback in order to evaluate and use it afterwards. This process does not mean a technocratic procedure that jumps back from the output to the input and creates a simple cause–effect loop. Similarly, this process has nothing to do with a behaviorist view of the consequences of behavior, such as praise, encouragement, or negative and positive reinforcement. In the understanding of Visible Learning, feedback is about how learners and teachers talk about learning and teaching and how they can share information about it. So it's about their interpretations!

Therefore, the focus of successful feedback is not so much on quantity as on the quality of feedback. Learners must be taught to understand feedback, give feedback, and receive feedback. Teachers should also be taught to ask their learners to listen and reflect, and to use the new perspective they have gained to work better with students. Feedback leads to a trusting atmosphere between learners and teachers, and to a climate in which all participants can talk freely about what they do not know, where their mistakes and misconceptions lie, what their strengths and weaknesses are. Effective feedback sees mistakes as opportunities and challenges for learning.

Surely it would be wonderful if all of us could regulate ourselves well. But each of us finds ourselves in situations that challenge us, where we don't have an answer and we need experts to help us ensure that we can see clearly what the next step is. Some of us are willing to experiment, hypothesize, try different solutions and take responsibility – but these are the skills we need to teach if we want to help students to become their own teachers and to optimize feedback on the question "What is the next step?"

I have worked with Klaus Zierer and got to know his research team in Germany. He and his team are dedicated to feedback. This book attempts to shed light on feedback from the perspective of "What is the next step?" It aims to help teachers to obtain feedback on their impact and thus to see more clearly what they are doing for their students.

Melbourne, 19 March 2018

John Hattie

CHAPTER

1

Introduction

Feedback between desire and reality

We cannot say that there is no public interest in schooling and education. Every week, this is demonstrated in the daily press, where ideas and plans for educational reforms are discussed regularly and controversially by all kind of experts and alleged experts. It is surprising that these discussions do not always find their way into school staff rooms.

Why do so many people talk about teaching, but teachers themselves talk so little about it?

Bill Gates (who not a teacher but is interested in and committed to educational policy) concludes: "We all need people who will give us feedback – that's how we improve professionally. But unfortunately, there is one group of people who get almost no systematic feedback to help them do their jobs better – teachers."[1]

Teachers often lack systematic feedback and, as a consequence, don't talk about teaching. You may quickly be inclined to object: "That's not true! We talk a lot!" This is beyond doubt: Teachers talk a lot about parents, students, colleagues, school administrators, the curriculum, and assessment. On average, however, they talk little about their lessons, the goals they pursue, the content they want to convey, the methods they choose, and the media they use. This reality is contrasted with numerous research studies that demonstrate how important feedback is in the classroom and how effective it is for students' achievement. In this context, John Hattie's work, known as Visible Learning (Hattie, 2008, 2013; Hattie & Zierer, 2017), should be mentioned first and foremost. Starting with Hattie's work, the call for feedback to find its way into schools and lessons is more than understandable. If teachers talk more about students, the curricula, and assessment than about teaching and the impact of their teaching during a school week, then there is a need for action.

Is feedback something between desire and reality? In view of this area of tension, it is not surprising that in recent years several school development processes have been initiated to implement feedback in everyday teaching. The authors of this book both first worked at entirely different places to strengthen feedback in schools before joining forces through contact with John Hattie and have been cooperating since then (see Wisniewski & Zierer, 2017).

Benedikt Wisniewski: In 2012, when I was working as a school psychologist and teacher, I began to systematically use feedback questionnaires to reflect on my own teaching and to observe the lessons of teacher trainees. As profitable as this was, I found that paper–pencil processes – simply because of the enormous amount of time they take – are useless for this purpose. So I started working on a digital solution. As a co-developer of www.feedbackschule.de (English beta version, www.visiblefeedback.com), a system for app-based instructional feedback, I focused on the implementation of feedback in schools.

Klaus Zierer: I have become more and more aware of the importance of feedback both in practice and in research, especially through the transfer of John Hattie's work to the German-speaking world. In the meantime, a large number of other contributions have been made, most recently with John Hattie in *10 Mindframes for Visible Learning* (2017). Not least for this reason, I received a request from the Bavarian State Ministry of Education and Science, as well as from the State Institute for School Quality and Educational Research, to participate in a pilot project called "Student feedback during practical teacher training."

There are many reasons why feedback has not (yet) made it to schools. In the light of our experience in recent years, we can name three:

1. Teachers are still socialized as "lone wolves." This begins during teacher training at the university, where cooperative forms of learning occur, but usually not as a form of examination. In the same way, it also extends into the second phase of teacher training, which everyone has to do on their own. Teachers don't learn to cooperate and to give each other feedback.

2. Teachers frequently lack the necessary skills and mindframes. Teachers neither learn how effective feedback is given and asked

for, nor do they receive systematic support in terms of their mindframes on these issues.

3. Structurally speaking, there is hardly any time and space for feedback in the classroom. Competence and mindframes alone are not enough to enable feedback successfully. If they are present, however, a corresponding framework can become very important.

With this book, we will certainly not be able to dispel all the concerns we have heard about feedback. But our hope is to make a contribution that will increase the number of teachers championing the cause of feedback. In this respect, we will pursue three objectives:

1. First, we will shed light on the broad and complex field in the scope of feedback from the perspective of educational science.
2. Second, we will discuss a form of feedback that has emerged as one of the most effective in research: feedback that teachers get from students.
3. Third, we want to show that successful feedback is not just a question of using a technology that requires certain competencies. Rather, current studies indicate that successful feedback is based on a professional mindframe.

With these goals in mind, we have structured the book as follows.

Chapter 2 begins with an overview of the current state of research about feedback, especially the research presented by John Hattie and Klaus Zierer in *10 Mindframes for Visible Learning* (2017). We are not interested in depicting the scientific discourse in its entirety. This would fail to reach the target audience of teachers. Instead, we try to focus on the essentials for the practical implementation of feedback in the classroom.

In Chapter 3 we discuss the reasons for student feedback (feedback given to teachers by learners), the advantages, and – more specifically – what it has to do with good teaching.

Chapter 4 focuses on student feedback from a practical teaching point of view: from the task of finding the right questions through effective collection of data to professional discussion and implementation of changes. In this context, we consider both the perspective of the feedback recipient and the perspective of the feedback provider. We show that the relevance of feedback is closely linked to the use of instruments that provide objective, reliable, and valid results. We outline psychological processes that can occur after one has received feedback and then illustrate how change processes can take place by means of practical examples.

In Chapter 5 we discuss the progressive combination of digitization and feedback. Using examples generated with the Visible Feedback software (www.visiblefeedback.com), we show how the acquisition and evaluation of student feedback can benefit from a digital solution. We use typical feedback scenarios and practices described in Chapter 4 to explain how feedback can work in practice.

Chapter 6 focuses on how feedback can become more than a tool for individual teachers, but it can also change an entire school. We shed some light on the dazzling concept of "feedback culture" and show how it relates to pedagogical professionalism.

Note

1 www.wucftv.org/blogs/american-graduate/ted-talks-education-teachers-need-real-feedback/

Bibliography

Hattie, J. (2008). *Visible learning: A synthesis of over 800 meta-analyses relating to achievement*. London: Routledge.

Hattie, J. (2013). *Visible learning for teachers*. London: Routledge.

Hattie, J., & Zierer, K. (2017). *10 mindframes for visible learning: Teaching for success*. London: Routledge.

Wisniewski, B., & Zierer, K. (2017). *Visible feedback: Ein Leitfaden für erfolgreiches Unterrichtsfeedback*. Baltmannsweiler: Schneider Hohengehren.

CHAPTER

2

Feedback in the light of Visible Learning

> You may be familiar with teachers' discussions about feedback from your own experience. Two camps can be identified quickly. While one side says, "Why should I ask students for their opinion? They don't know what to do anyway," the other side argues: "Absolutely indispensable! I can only improve my lessons if I get information from students or colleagues."
>
> Please reflect on your mindframe towards feedback:
>
> - What role does it play in your lessons?
> - Why do you use or not use certain feedback procedures?
> - What are your reasons for this?

A closer look at the discussion reveals that it is not always clear what people are talking about: there is not always consensus on what the word "feedback" means. Please also consider the following questions at this point:

- What do you understand by "feedback?"
- What types of feedback are there?
- When is feedback successful – and when is it not?
- Who gives and who receives feedback?
- What is a prerequisite for successful feedback?
- What skills and mindframes do you need as a teacher in order to be able to give and receive feedback successfully?

5

Feedback in the light of Visible Learning

We will answer these and similar questions in this chapter. It is deliberately not our aim to claim completeness. This chapter is not intended to be a scientific treatise. Rather, our aim is to draw attention to the topic of feedback from an educational-scientific point of view; to present the central results of educational research; and to stimulate a reflection on our readers' own roles, expectations, competencies, and mindframes. Ultimately, we would like to initiate a conversation about all of these.

For this purpose, the first section focuses on the question of educational research findings, with the following argument: For a long time, the educational discourse was dominated by experience, intuition, and something like a "gut feeling." Without wishing to disqualify these aspects, from an empirical point of view there are several findings which are worth taking into account in order to reflect on one's own experience, intuition, and feeling and to be able to question them critically and constructively. In the second section, in the light of an evidence-based approach, we will examine the factor feedback in more detail by comparing it with other factors. In the third section, we present detailed results from primary studies in order to explain the criteria for successful feedback.

Therefore, after reading this chapter you should be able to

- explain the core statements of evidence-based teaching from an educational research perspective;
- describe the feedback factor in the light of key research findings;
- distinguish different levels of feedback (self/personality, task, process, and self-regulation);
- explain the feedback perspectives of the past, present, and future; and
- discern different feedback providers and feedback recipients.

Evidence-based teaching

These considerations show that there is a lot of experience in the field of education, but unfortunately it is not always clear which experience is important and which is not. Thus, myths are born: "Open instruction is better than traditional instruction," "Teaching works better in smaller classes," and "The comprehensive school system is superior to the joint school system," to name just three examples.

> Please use Google Scholar or a similar Internet search engine to find studies on "homework," "teacher – student relationships," and "feedback" and take note of the number of search results. You'll quickly realize that we are not dealing with a lack of studies and the knowledge that goes with them. Rather, we are confronted with an almost unmanageable number of research results that could not be more different from each other. In this exercise, for example, you will find studies demonstrating that homework has little impact on student achievement – along with studies that show that homework has a major impact on student achievement. Which are correct?
>
> Similarly, you can make the following attempt: Go to a teaching staff room and ask your colleagues for the best way to teach. You will hardly receive one single answer to this question but instead five or six different answers, or perhaps even 10 or even more.

Scientific evidence is helpful to counteract myth making. Empirical science asks not only whether there is a significant correlation between two aspects but also how large that effect is. More than anything else, this approach is embodied in Visible Learning, the largest dataset of empirical educational research, which was compiled by John Hattie in the course of more than 15 years of collecting and interpreting data (cf. Hattie, 2008, 2012; Hattie & Zierer, 2017; Zierer, 2014).

More than 800 meta-analyses form the basis of Hattie's synthesis, comprising about 80,000 individual primary studies in which approximately 250 million learners have participated. It is important to mention these numbers: If one compares them, for example, with the numbers of PISA, which has massively influenced worldwide educational policy in recent years, the immense scope of Visible Learning becomes evident. After all, PISA comprises only around six million learners.

Visible Learning attempts to use a synthesis of meta-analyses to get a grip on the multitude of educational science research results and to culminate in core messages. From the underlying meta-analyses, 150 factors have been generated, including "class size," "teacher – student relationships," "direct instruction," and "feedback." An effect size is determined for each factor. If the effect size is positive, it means that the factor leads to an increase in student achievement, and if it is negative, the factor leads to a reduction in student achievement. If we take this naive but quite correct premise for the interpretation of effect sizes and put it in relation to the frequency with which these effect sizes were found in the numerous meta-analyses, we get the following illustration (Figure 2.1, cf. Zierer, 2014 and Hattie & Zierer, 2017).

It is immediately apparent that almost everything that happens in classrooms leads to an increase in academic achievement. In other words, in 90% to 95% of cases, students leave school smarter than they were when they entered. That could reassure us teachers, but it shouldn't. This only makes it clear that people always learn: "Anything works." For example, both introducing a new curriculum and keeping an old curriculum will have a positive effect. Or, to take another example, one will achieve a positive effect whether one transforms the school system into a one-tier, two-, three-, four-, or five-tier system. To put it in a nutshell: it is difficult to prevent student achievement.

Starting from these findings, the crucial question in Visible Learning is not to simply ask whether the effect size of a factor is positive or negative. Rather, Hattie argues that the zero point should be at 0.4. Why 0.4? This value represents the average of all collected effect sizes and marks the range of "desired effects." It is usually compared with the average gain in achievement during one school year. Consequently, the requirement that should be pursued is simple but convincing: better than the average! Consider this: Everyone makes progress simply by aging. This is called the "development effect" and it is characterized by effect sizes between zero and 0.2. Values between 0.2 and 0.4 can be described as ordinary "school attendance effects" that occur in an average school, with an average teacher, in an average class, and supported by an average home. Negative values that appear to

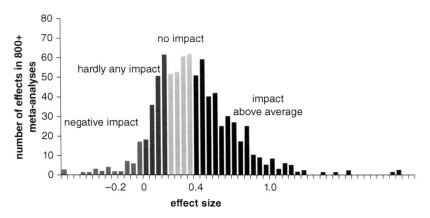

FIGURE 2.1 Distribution of all effect sizes observed in Visible Learning

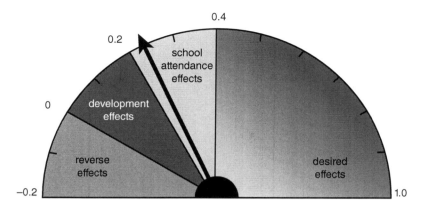

FIGURE 2.2 Effect size of the "class size" factor

be particularly problematic are identified as "reverse effects." They are very rare but not less interesting. Effect sizes can be illustrated by a barometer (Figure 2.2).

In the rest of this chapter, we use these considerations to argue that effect sizes are an indicator for importance. Nonetheless, it should always be borne in mind that factors with low effect sizes can be interesting too. In order to increase a factor's effect, it is often necessary to understand why a factor that appears to be important actually has little impact on student learning. Accordingly, it is essential to understand empirical data if one wishes to make it fruitful for teaching practice.

Feedback as an effective factor

What do we know about the "feedback" factor? How much research is there? What effect size can we calculate for it, and how effective is it in comparison to other factors?

First of all, from an educational research point of view, feedback has become increasingly important in recent years. Figure 2.3 compares the frequency of citation of the terms "feedback" and "behaviorism" in PsycINFO, one of the most important international databases of empirical educational research, from 1964 to 2008:

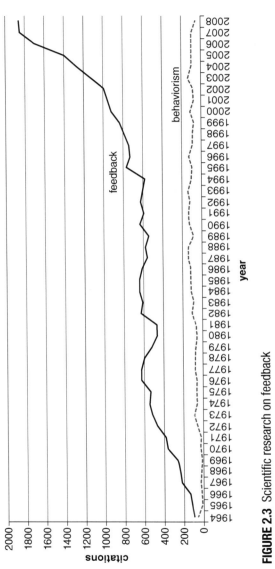

FIGURE 2.3 Scientific research on feedback

Similarly, a search in FIS education, the German-language educational research information system, leads to the conclusion that since 2002, more and more German-language publications on feedback have been published: in 2002 there were six publications; in 2012 there were 29 publications. It is not surprising that the factor feedback plays an important role in Visible Learning: Apart from "computer-assisted instruction" and "gender," it is the third most frequently investigated factor. It has the greatest effect size of these three factors and therefore ranks much higher when the 150 factors from Visible Learning are compared (see Table 2.1).

These results can be illustrated as shown in Figure 2.4 (see Zierer, 2014, p. 65).

The scope of feedback research clearly shows that it is not trivial to distinguish successful feedback from less successful feedback. Teachers are right to answer the question whether they give a lot of feedback with "yes." Teachers *give* a lot of feedback every day – and the smaller the classes are, the more feedback they give. Thus, one would be inclined to conclude that a reduction in class size alone would lead to an immense improvement of teacher feedback and thus in student achievement. However, none of this is true. Successful feedback is not a question of quantity but of quality. Again, the Visible Learning research (cf. also Hattie & Timperley, 2007) is helpful to show the differences involved.

It is necessary to clarify what the term "feedback" actually means and under which conditions feedback is successful.

Definition of feedback

The lowest common denominator of the numerous attempts at defining feedback in scientific literature may be seen in the following proposal.

TABLE 2.1 Most frequently studied factors

FACTOR	NUMBER OF META-ANALYSES	EFFECT SIZE	RANK
Gender	81	0.37	77
Computer-assisted instruction	41	0.12	133
Feedback	23	0.75	10

Feedback in the light of Visible Learning

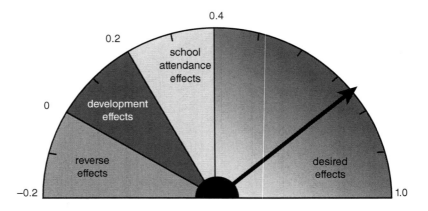

FIGURE 2.4 Effect size of the "feedback" factor

> Feedback is a data-based exchange of information between people.

Since feedback can also be found in non-school and extracurricular contexts, "classroom feedback" can be defined as a special form given and received by different people. It is important to distinguish between

- feedback from learners to teachers (student feedback);
- feedback from teachers to learners (teacher feedback); and
- feedback from teachers to teachers (collegial feedback) (see Figure 2.5).

Fortunately, this working definition is sufficient for determining the criteria for successful feedback.

Criteria for successful feedback

On the basis of this working definition, there are three questions that must be answered in order to provide information as to when feedback can be particularly effective:

Feedback in the light of Visible Learning

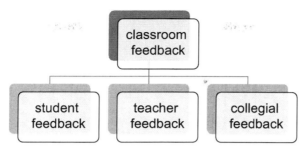

FIGURE 2.5 Types of feedback in schools

1 What data are required for successful feedback?
2 What is the focus of successful feedback?
3 Who gives and who receives successful feedback?

Let's start with the first question: What data are required for successful feedback?

What data are required for successful feedback?

For a long time, people in the educational context believed that to know for sure what works and what does not we just need to collect enough data. The result is a large pool of data that has been collected but has not interpreted. In this respect, one of the core statements in Visible Learning is that we should not collect more data but instead should properly interpret the data that we already have.

In terms of feedback, this means that we don't necessarily need to collect more data to implement successful feedback in classrooms. We already have *a lot* of data! We just have to see teaching through the eyes of our students and reflect on what we do. If we understand "evidence-based teaching" as an effort to search for clues that confirm the impact of our thinking and our actions, then a number of important sources of data for feedback are already available, including the observation of a group work phase, an exercise book entry, a student's question, a student's answer, a failed experiment, a successful teacher's lecture, the results of an assignment, and many more.

Ideally, the evidence collected in this way is complemented by the evidence collected in educational science, and both forms of evidence are interchanged. The search for one's own impact combined with the experiences of colleagues as well as the results of educational research is a characteristic of pedagogical expertise.

The second question: What is the focus of successful feedback?

What is the focus of successful feedback?

It is precisely in this context that the results of Visible Learning are vital, because they provide a series of hints for best teaching practice. It is important to understand that feedback can be given at different levels (Figure 2.6, cf. Hattie & Zierer, 2017).

Feedback at the level of self/personality

Feedback at the level of self/personality focuses on the personal characteristics of the student. This includes praise and criticism, for example: "You're great!" "You're a hard-working person!" or "You're a good student/teacher!" This type of feedback has a minimal effect on student achievement. Why? Because feedback at the level of the self does not contain any information about behavior that can be modified: it has to do almost exclusively with personality traits that are difficult or impossible to change. Feedback at this level may even lead to negative effects, because students perceive it as an evaluation of their own person. For example, excessive praise can reduce motivation to take risks, because feedback recipients are loath to jeopardize their positive self-image. In the same way, criticism that is directed at the person rather than the error can lead to a negative self-image. Feedback at the level of the self is especially problematic if the student already has high intrinsic motivation. In that situation feedback provides extrinsic motivation – and in

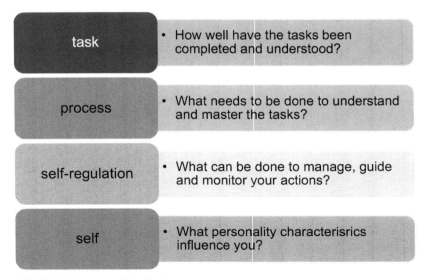

FIGURE 2.6 Levels of feedback

a worst-case scenario, could reduce the recipient's intrinsic motivation. From a psychological point of view, it is much worse to be motivated by external praise rather than by the enjoyment of doing something. Learning is more effective and sustainable if people have a high level of intrinsic motivation. A prime example of this type of feedback is the practice of rewarding students with sweets for proper and disciplined work: sweets are not only unhealthy, but from an educational point of view this practice is poisonous to intrinsic motivation. Similarly, it is dangerous to overload students with stickers or tokens. This form of feedback is purely extrinsic and can, in the worst case, replace an intrinsic motivation.

Feedback on the level of the self can, however, be important for the teacher–student relationship, where it can have positive effects. However, note that the students' starting point of the learning situation must be taken into consideration. Nevertheless, there are far more effective ways of creating an atmosphere of security, confidence, and trust in this context. All in all, the research is consistent: feedback at the level of the self should be used in a well-dosed and well-considered manner. Often, less is more.

In contrast to feedback at the level of self/personality, feedback relating to task, process, and self-regulation are connected to a student's performance. The impact of feedback at these levels is both more positive and has different outcomes.

Feedback at the task level

With feedback at the task level, the student receives feedback for the product of his or her performance. For example, in a test, the achievement of learning objectives is measured by student success in completing different tasks. After the student has completed the test, the teacher indicates which tasks were completed correctly or incorrectly. In this way, the learner gets information on *what* he or she can and cannot do.

Feedback at the process level

With feedback at the process level, a student receives feedback on the effort and/or skill involved in his or her performance. For example, the teacher can review a test with regard to performance and determine whether the test reveals a speedy working process, whether there are signs of sloppiness, and whether many careless mistakes can be detected, to name just a few. In this case, the learner receives information about *how* he or she has worked.

Feedback at the level of self-regulation

With feedback at the level of self-regulation, a student receives feedback about the control mechanisms of his or her performance. For example, a student can be told after a test how he or she has managed to focus his or her attention, implement time-management strategies, and apply self-monitoring during the test. Thus, the learner receives information on how he or she has regulated the product and the process of his or her performance.

Please reflect on a situation in which a colleague visits your classroom to observe your teaching and to discuss the lesson afterwards. What kind of feedback would you like? Would you prefer feedback at the task level that shows you what you did correctly or incorrectly? Would you like feedback on the level of your personality, telling you what your counterpart noticed about your character? Feedback at the process level that shows you how effective your planning process was and how to evaluate your planning documents? Or feedback at the level of self-regulation that shows you what you can work on to deliver the next lesson more effectively?

We have surveyed hundreds of learners to ask which form they would prefer. The result is always the same: The clear majority would like to receive feedback at the level of self-regulation, while only very few would ask for feedback at the level of the task or process. From the learner's point of view – and note that you are also a learner in our example reflection – feedback at the level of self-regulation is most desired.

In contrast to the feedback learners wish to receive, the feedback they actually get in classrooms on a daily basis is mainly at the task level (Table 2.2, cf. Hattie & Zierer, 2017):

TABLE 2.2 Percentage of different types of feedback in the classroom

	HATTIE & MASTERS (2011)	VAN DEN BERGH, ROS, & BEIJAARD (2010)	GAN (2011)
Level	18 high school classes	32 middle school teachers	235 peers
Task	59%	51%	70%
Process	25%	42%	25%
Self-regulation	2%	2%	1%
Self	14%	5%	4%

Feedback in the light of Visible Learning

Learners rarely get the feedback they want and need most; instead, they are provided with the forms of feedback they find least important. How much could be achieved simply by making teachers more reflective of the feedback they give so often?

In this context, it is also clear that successful feedback is not a question of quantity but of quality: What good is it for a learner, for example, if the teacher repeatedly points out his or her mistakes, but without providing concrete information on what caused the mistake and how it can be avoided in the future? In other words, more feedback at the task level alone is not especially effective. Only when combined with feedback at the process and self-regulation levels can it become effective (Figure 2.7, cf. Hattie & Zierer, 2017).

Some of what has been said so far may seem self-evident, but it isn't. When class size is reduced by five or 10 learners, for example, the amount of feedback given on the self-regulation level does not automatically increase. Teachers with smaller classes give more feedback, but most of it is at the already dominant levels of task and process. What good is it for the learner to be told not just five but 10 times that he or she has made a mistake? A greater impact cannot be achieved this way, which explains why the effect size of class size reduction is only 0.21. This makes a central finding from Visible Learning clear: Learners do not need more of the same. They need something else.

It would be wrong to give the impression that one level of feedback is somehow better than the others. Rather, the core message is that the various feedback levels interlock and interact. In this respect, it is not only a matter of finding the right level of feedback but also of giving complete

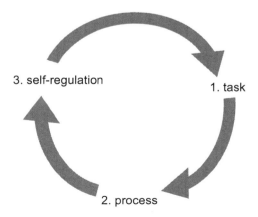

FIGURE 2.7 Feedback on three levels

feedback – in other words, feedback that focuses on the levels of task, process, and self-regulation. It is not helpful to provide feedback on the personality because this form open up any opportunities for change.

These considerations lead to three central insights into successful feedback: First, each of the levels mentioned carries risks. Above all, over- and under-challenge should be mentioned in this context. Second, when used exclusively, each level runs the risk of being incomplete and resulting in missing information and monotony. And third, the effectiveness of each level increases to the extent that it is connected to the other levels. The whole is more than the sum of its parts.

Bearing this in mind, considering the performance level of the learners is crucial to determine the proportion of feedback they need on each level. Consider the following example.

> Imagine a novice learner who is completely new to a certain domain. He or she does not yet have any insight into the matter, knows no connections, and does not (yet) understand the basic elements. Take a first-grader as an illustration, who is just getting to know the numeral space from 1 to 20: What level of feedback does he or she need? And now compare this feedback with the feedback you would give to an expert in his field. He or she knows about the details in the area, knows about pitfalls, and has already developed deeper insights. Take for example Tiger Woods, Roger Federer, or Thomas Müller: What level of feedback do they need to improve?

It is pretty obvious that novices need different feedback than do experts. While novices must first know what they are doing wrong, and therefore need feedback at the task level, experts need feedback at the self-regulation level. The novice from the current example may not know that $3 + 6 = 8$ is wrong. How could he? In contrast, an expert usually knows all too well what he or she is doing wrong: Tiger Woods knows that he hit the ball in the rough, Roger Federer knows that his serve was not in the field, and Thomas Müller knows that his penalty kick went far beyond the goal. They need feedback to use this mistake to manage their learning processes.

Consequently, the higher the learner's level of achievement, the more feedback at the level of self-regulation is necessary, but without becoming exclusive: Complete feedback is better for both novices and experts. Novices need more feedback on the task level but also some feedback on the process level and self-regulation level. Experts need more feedback at the level of self-regulation but also some feedback at the level of task and process. Feedback is a complex didactic tool for controlling and optimizing learning processes; as such, it is related to other aspects of successful teaching.

In addition to distinguishing between feedback levels, Visible Learning (see also Hattie & Timperley, 2007) explains that each of these levels can be served from three perspectives: "feed-up," "feed-back," and "feed-forward." This allows us to introduce a further dimension of feedback that shows how complex this seemingly self-evident factor is.

Feed-up compares the actual status with a target status. It is thus related to the present.

Feed-back compares the actual status with a previous status. In this respect, it focuses on the past.

Feed-forward explains the target status on the basis of the actual status. It is therefore directed towards the future.

When discussing a test with a student, the teacher can provide information at the task level: first, on which tasks have been solved correctly and which haven't to compare the current status to the target status (feed-up); second, on how the learner's current performance level has changed compared to the last test, where he or she has improved, and where he or she hasn't, comparing the current status to the previous test (feed-back); and third, on which tasks the learner has to put work into in the future (feed-forward).

Successful feedback can be seen from the perspectives of the past, present, and future. All three are interconnected and together form a comprehensive picture. It becomes clear that present-related feedback is based on past feedback and can be seen as a precursor to future-oriented feedback.

Visible Learning repeatedly emphasizes that it is important for successful feedback to be as complete as possible. But what does complete feedback look like? Which areas need to be considered? How can feedback levels and perspectives be connected? Although one of the greatest merits of Visible Learning is that it pays increased attention to feedback, many things remain unclear in practice, which is why the following attempt is made to combine levels and perspectives of feedback into a feedback matrix (Table 2.3, cf. Hattie & Zierer, 2017).

TABLE 2.3 Feedback matrix

LEVELS OF FEEDBACK

		TASK	PROCESS	SELF-REGULATION
Perspectives of feedback	**Past** (feed-back)	Where is progress in terms of objectives and content?	Where is there progress in terms of service provision? Are there any indications of better processing?	Where does progress appear to be taking place with regard to the strategies of self-regulation?
	Present (feed-up)	What objectives have been achieved? Which contents were understood?	How was the service rendered? Are there any instructions for editing?	Which strategies of self-regulation have been used successfully?
	Future (feed-forward)	What are the next goals to set? Which contents are to be set next?	What information on the provision of services is to be given next?	Which strategies of self-regulation should be applied next?

Returning to the third question in the "Criteria for successful feedback" section: Who gives and who receives successful feedback?

Who gives and who receives successful feedback?

With regard to the persons involved, it is basically possible to speak of a feedback provider and a feedback recipient (Figure 2.8).

Often the discussion of feedback is dominated by the idea that it is directed from the teacher to the learner (Figure 2.9). This is accompanied by an assignment to the teacher to provide feedback to students as often as possible, as detailed as possible, and as intensively as possible. As important as this form of feedback is, it is only one of many and – in its exaggeration – runs the risk of being overused and degenerating into a pointless exercise involving never-ending verbal comments on the learning progress of the students. Reports that are read only by the

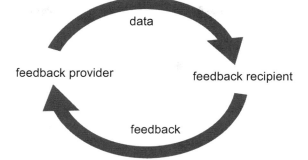

FIGURE 2.8 Feedback provider and feedback recipient

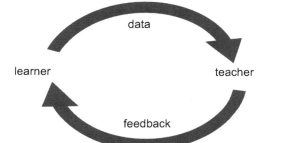

FIGURE 2.9 Feedback from teacher to learner

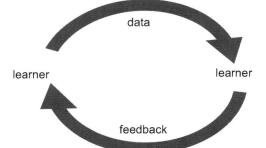

FIGURE 2.10 Feedback from learners to learners

teacher and the school administration may be an exaggerated example of this. It cannot be the aim to give every learner complete feedback in every lesson. What the goal can and must be, however, is to know that there are different levels of feedback and to use them as often as possible on the basis of the initial learning situation.

Further forms of feedback become the focus of attention. Especially in open learning environments, feedback from learners to learners is sometimes praised as a pedagogical revolution (Figure 2.10).

Against this backdrop, one of the results of feedback research that is cited in Visible Learning is certainly one of the most compelling. According to a study by Graham A. Nuthall (2007), the majority of the feedback that learners give each other is incorrect. In a superficial interpretation, this calls into question feedback from learners to learners as well as feedback from learners to teachers: How could a student give a teacher reasonable feedback?

Considering the complexity of feedback, it should be clear that it requires certain competencies: students, for example, must be made aware of the difference between the levels of task, process, and self-regulation and must develop appropriate skills in speaking and listening. Providing feedback needs to be learned – and since humans learn a lot from role models, the teacher should play a central role in this context.

We should not forget the question of mindframes. It is often the case that feedback is incorrect. For example, out of consideration for my friend, I don't tell him what's not going well. Because of prevailing group pressure, I do not point out any difficulties. Addressing this is a major challenge. Successful feedback requires a combination of special competences and mindframes. When students are taught these competences and mindframes, learner–learner feedback can be effectively integrated into lessons. Moreover, perspectives and levels also apply to teachers and, in this respect, to feedback from teachers to teachers (Figure 2.11).

We sometimes believe that fully trained teachers have reached a level of perfection. Of course, they haven't, and they are on the path of getting better and on the path of developing competence and mindframes as feedback providers and feedback recipients. The latter becomes particularly important when it comes to the question of whether students are allowed to provide feedback about teaching at all. It is obvious that this is not entirely possible. Nonetheless it is also a sign of expertise if a teacher can use student feedback, regardless of the quality, in order to draw conclusions about the teaching process and self-regulation.

Particularly in times of educational policy challenges – and especially now with growing issues of inclusion and migration – efforts are made to decrease the learner–teacher ratio and thus require higher investments in education. The argument often used here is that if you do not invest in education now, you will need to spend much more later on. At first glance, it is difficult to contradict this argument. Both increasing financial resources and investing in teachers is in line with the core messages formulated in Visible Learning. But a second look warns against stopping the discussion at this point. What is also pointed

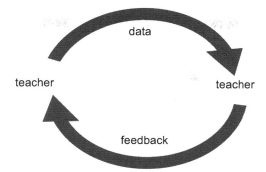

FIGURE 2.11 Feedback from teachers to teachers

out in Visible Learning is the fact that investing money alone cannot be the answer and not all teachers are successful on their own initiative but need to acquire certain competencies and mindframes.

Successful feedback is not only a question of knowledge and skill. It is essentially a question of will and values. The appropriate competence and mindframe are required. As important as all the constellations of feedback from teachers to learners are for successful learning processes and as effective as they can be in the ideal case, they cannot provide the most important form of feedback.

Feedback from learners to the teacher

More important than feedback from the teacher to the learner, from the learner to the learner, or from the teacher to the teacher is the feedback from the learner to the teacher (student feedback; Figure 2.12).

Why is this form of feedback so important? Questions as to whether the educational goals have been achieved, whether the content has been understood, whether the teaching methods were useful, and whether the media have been helpful can be answered by teachers only from an observer's perspective. It is the learners who can comment directly on these questions. They are the ones who can make learning visible.

Quite often, teachers will leave the classroom and report that they are satisfied because everything seems to have gone well, while students report that they did what they were told simply to avoid being penalized, and that they had been bored during class. This strategy is called "gaming the system." Please keep in mind that only 20% of what happens in the classroom can be observed through external assessment; 80% of the events are not recognizable at first glance and have to be made visible. One way to do this is by eliciting student

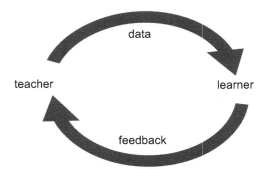

FIGURE 2.12 Feedback from learners to teachers

self-assessments. The difference between external assessment and self-assessment is therefore important. External assessment can only be achieved through dialogue. Those teachers who rely exclusively on their own impressions run the risk of not reaching their students. To plan effective lessons, teachers need to ask students questions about goals, content, methods, and media.

Meaningful and successful feedback from learners to teachers has nothing to do with assessing teachers. Anyone who argues in this way has either not understood the meaning of feedback or holds convictions that are more than problematic. One thing must become clear to critics of student feedback: Students are not there for teachers; teachers are there for students. For teachers to be able to help learners in the best possible way, teaching cannot and must not be a one-way street. The motto that many children learn all too quickly, "One speaks and everyone else listens," must be discarded. Unfortunately, many children simply go to school to watch teachers at work.

Successful feedback is a circular process consisting of feedback from teachers to students and feedback from students to teachers. Since the two forms are structurally related and mutually dependent, it is possible to speak of an infinite dialogue. Teaching is thus a dialogue, an interaction between people who are on a common path, who work together and celebrate successes together, but also fail, make mistakes, exchange ideas, and look through each other's eyes. All this is only possible if feedback is part of the lessons.

Culture of errors

It should be clear from the remarks made so far that a central aspect of successful feedback is to be seen in the culture of errors: Are mistakes seen as something to be avoided, or are mistakes seen as necessary to the learning process? Learning means making mistakes – and teaching too, by the way.

If errors are something negative and unwanted, the decision is made quickly. At the same time, teachers waste a variety of opportunities for their students to learn, resulting in a reductionistic understanding of mistakes. It is never the error that is the problem. But if errors are seen as problems, communication about the error can be problematic. Just as it is problematic to merely draw a students' attention to mistakes – and thus to make accusations unilaterally at the task level – it is also questionable to not mention errors at all. Students often know where they have made mistakes but often do not dare to talk about them. If teachers do not address their own mistakes either, a culture emerges in which mistakes are concealed. How can mistakes be communicated in a way that is both thoughtful and conducive to learning?

Here too, the levels of feedback are helpful: It is problematic when factual errors in the learning process are combined with feedback at the level of the self. Then, especially with younger learners, the impression of being a bad person and failing to learn can easily be developed. This can occur, for example, if a previously frequently given feedback is no longer given. For example, if a learner is regaled with "Great!" and "Bravo!" – a response that learners perceive as feedback at the level of the self – a lack of this feedback can negatively affect the learner's self-esteem. In the worst case, fear can arise. In this respect, learners should always be made aware of the level to which the feedback relates. For example, the teacher could, when handing a workbook to a primary student, make it clear that he or she appreciates and likes the student but that the student has made a mistake on the task that has certain causes and can be handled in the future. The teacher may encourage the child to ask for help, and make him/herself available for further inquiries.

The feedback from the learner to the teacher is analogous: If a teacher receives feedback from students that a certain part of a particular lesson was not easy to understand or was boring, this refers to the process and has a completely different effect than feedback on the level of self ("You are a bad teacher."). The feedback can then be used to improve what didn't go so well.

According to numerous empirical research results, feedback has proved to be an extremely effective factor in terms of student achievement. Feedback is diverse. It is particularly effective when it relates to the levels of process and self-regulation and when given to the teacher by students.

Bibliography

Gan, J. (2011). *The effects of prompts and explicit coaching on peer feedback quality* (Dissertation, University of Auckland).

Hattie, J. (2008). *Visible learning: A synthesis of over 800 meta-analyses relating to achievement.* London: Routledge.

Hattie, J. (2012). *Visible learning for teachers: Maximizing impact on learning.* London: Routledge.

Hattie, J., & Zierer, K. (2017). *10 mindframes for visible learning: Teaching for success.* London: Routledge.

Hattie, J., & Timperley, H. (2007). The power of feedback. *Review of Educational Research, 77*(1), 81–112.

Hattie, J., & Masters, D. (2011). *Visible learning plus.* Supporting Material, Visible Learning Workshop presentation in Adelaide, South Australia.

Nuthall, G. (2007). *The hidden lives of learners.* Wellington: Nzcer Press.

Van den Bergh, L., Ros, A., & Beijaard, D. (2010). *Feedback van basisschoolleerkrachten tijdens actief leren. de huidige praktijk* (ORD-paper, ORD, Enschede).

Zierer, K. (2014). *Hattie für gestresste Lehrer: Kernbotschaften und Handlungsempfehlungen aus John Hatties "Visible Learning"" und "Visible Learning for Teachers".* Baltmannsweiler: Schneider Hohengehren.

CHAPTER

3

Student feedback

One of teachers' core tasks is to explain and make things clear. This is what they have studied and practiced in compulsory internships and training programs as well as in many years of professional experience. So why should these teaching professionals ask their students what they could do better?
How would you answer this question?

Having shown how feedback works in Chapter 2, we now take a closer look at a form that has proven to be particularly effective: student feedback. We will point out reasons for this kind of feedback and take a stand on common myths and misconceptions. Since the public discourse on student feedback is characterized by misunderstandings of objectives, and all too often by confusion with teacher evaluation or professional assessment, these concepts will be separated from each other. Finally, we will highlight the role of student feedback as a driving force behind a teacher's professional development.

After reading this chapter, you should

- know arguments for student feedback,
- be able to comment on common myths regarding student feedback,
- be able to differentiate feedback from formal teacher evaluation, assessment, and rating; and
- know the role of student feedback in the development of instructional quality.

In 2007, the German Internet platform spickmich.de was founded by three Cologne university students. Students could rate their teachers and schools on this website. Within a very short time, more than

800,000 students registered on spickmich.de. Teachers could be graded anonymously in categories such as "professional competence," "motivation," "popularity," "clothing," "fair examinations," and "physical appearance." After a certain number of ratings per teacher, the results were made publicly accessible. In 2014, due to several teacher complaints, spickmich.de was shut down.

Spickmich.de is an example of the misuse (or even abuse) of feedback, because

- some of the evaluation criteria were not relevant to teaching (e.g., clothing);
- the evaluation criteria included areas that could not or only insufficiently be assessed by students (e.g., professional competence);
- the feedback results were made public; and
- the feedback was primarily aimed at exposure, not professional development.

Reasons for student feedback

"Why should I ask for feedback about my teaching? I'm a trained teacher, and I know best what works and what doesn't."

This statement by a colleague at one of our training events indicates that some people disagree on the question of whether teachers really need to get feedback from their students. While it is a natural part of everyday practice in other professional fields, feedback for teachers is usually limited to rare and spontaneous individual opinions and opinions of superiors in the context of official evaluation.

Our colleague's attitude of knowing best how good teaching works because she has professional expertise is not technically incorrect: Teachers are experts in teaching and have learned how to help students learn. However, the quoted colleague forgot one crucial factor: the students. Students are individuals, and something that works perfectly in one class can fail completely in another. Whether learners have understood something, how a certain method affected them, how exciting or boring they found something, or where they could no longer follow are things that only students can communicate. This has nothing to do with professional qualifications but simply relates to information that is exclusively accessible through feedback.

Take an example from a different job: A baker also knows which ingredients belong in a bread, how to knead the dough, and how long

Student feedback

to bake it. And yet, at the end of the day, the customers decide whether they like the taste of the bread or not.

As active directors of instruction, teachers have a very high impact on the success of their students' achievement. However, not all teachers have the same impact. Teaching is particularly effective when teachers try to see their instruction through the eyes of their students, when they try to understand how their teaching impacts their learners (Hattie, 2008). What does this mean in concrete terms?

In the professional context, there is certain relevant information that is not accessible to a person him or herself but to others. The "Johari window," named after its authors Joseph Luft and Harry Ingram (see Figure 3.1), illustrates how access to information works. It refers to information that is accessible to others but not to ourselves as a "blind spot." The only way to get access to this kind of information is feedback.

A classic blind spot for teachers is, for example, their estimation of the time they spend speaking in class. Helmke and colleagues (2013) were able to show that teachers' estimation of their speaking time during a lesson differs considerably from the time objectively measured. In short: Teachers talk way more than they think they do (Figure 3.2). In this sense, feedback offers the opportunity to reveal blind spots by comparing perspectives. The relevance of blind spots can range from minor to major – from the frequent repetition of a certain filler word and unfavorable non-verbal signals to content being presented too quickly or not clearly.

Student feedback can provide us with information about the impact of our own professional actions, which is important for the further

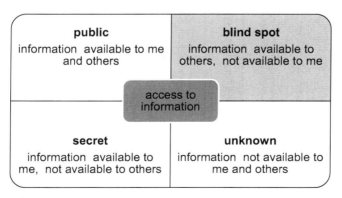

FIGURE 3.1 Johari window

Source: Luft and Ingram (1955).

Student feedback

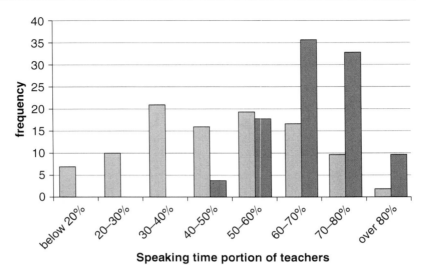

FIGURE 3.2 Speaking time by teachers in the classroom – estimation and actual measurement

Source: Helmke and Schrader (2013).

development of instructional quality. It also influences job satisfaction: Research clearly shows that feedback makes a significant contribution to the health of teachers. Enns and colleagues (2002) have been able to demonstrate that teachers who seek regular feedback in their professional practice

- feel that they are being encouraged as teachers;
- get more secure about their professional actions;
- put their own weaknesses into perspective;
- establish working partnerships;
- establish a research-oriented mindframe in the classroom;
- develop openness and sensitivity;
- have increased job satisfaction;
- experience reductions in stress;
- experience self-efficacy; and
- benefit from recognition and encouragement.

In this respect, student feedback is – contrary to frequent doubts – a supporting factor for teachers and, if you like, an essential pillar of teacher health.

Myths about student feedback

After outlining some reasons for student feedback, we now deal with negative mindframes. Often these arise from false assumptions, and unfortunately some of these misconceptions are widespread in staff rooms.

Myth 1: Student feedback has no significance whatsoever.

Student feedback has no significance only when teachers ask the wrong questions. Of course, the question "How did you like the lesson today" is a form of student feedback, but it does not provide any (or only very little) meaningful information. Usually, the objection to student feedback because of its low informative value is due to incorrect implementation and bad feedback instruments (see Chapter 4).

Myth 2: Feedback will be abused by students to pressure teachers.

This frequently voiced objection sometimes leads to great anxiety. Are students using feedback to get back at me? Are they just articulating their frustration? Are they attempting to pressure me? Teachers who obtain student feedback based on valid criteria consider the feedback from their students to be extremely fair (Ditton & Arnoldt, 2004). Abuse in the sense of unfair and offensive feedback or as a form of revenge is not what happens in reality (Feldman, 2007). In addition, abuse can be ruled out if one clearly distinguishes feedback from any kind of career-relevant assessment (see Chapter 3).

Myth 3: Student feedback makes teachers give better grades.

There are widespread concerns that interactions with students and, above all, the evaluation of performance will change due to a reciprocal relationship (in the manner of "If you give me positive feedback, then I'll give you good grades!"). Feedback from students to teachers does not influence how teachers grade their students (Aleamoni, 1999; Feldman, 2007).

Myth 4: Student feedback requires additional time and effort.

Complex paper–pencil instruments do require a lot of additional effort. However, there is no need for these because digital solutions have been available for years. These tools allow detailed and meaningful feedback without needing more than a few minutes of time, and they free teachers from the task of processing data (e.g., see Chapter 6).

Myth 5: Students cannot provide information on instructional quality. They lack maturity and pedagogical knowledge.

As a rule, student feedback about teaching coincides to a high degree both with the perceptions of colleagues and with the self-perception of the feedback recipient (Peterson, 2000, 2004; Irving, 2004). This is precisely why deviations of student feedback from teacher self-estimations are particularly interesting. Students cannot (and should not) provide feedback about didactic intricacies, since they are not experts in this field – but the point is that they don't have to. Student feedback refers to aspects of teaching that do not require specialist knowledge. Even primary school children can adequately give valid feedback on key indicators of the quality of teaching (Lenske, 2016).

Myth 6: Teachers themselves know best whether their lessons were good or not.

Self-estimations of the quality of one's own work have very low reliability (Zempel & Moser, 2005). On the contrary, a high amount of feedback leads to a significantly higher concordance between self-perception and objective assessment (ibid.), meaning that feedback leads to a more realistic self-perception. It is also well known that – no matter the field – most people rate their own abilities higher than those of the average person (known as the "above-average effect"). No one is immune to this misperception with regard to their own teaching. Self-perception is not sufficient to see whether one's work is truly above average. A realistic self-image is always based on a high degree of feedback.

Myth 7: Good teaching depends on the teacher's personality. Since personality traits are stable, feedback on teaching characteristics is pointless.

An overemphasis on largely unchangeable and unlearnable personality traits in explaining the quality of professional practice is evident in both beginners and experienced teachers (Bromme & Haag, 2004). However, empirical research clearly shows that the concept of "the born teacher" is outdated. Unchangeable characteristics are not a primary influence on the quality of teaching but rather professional knowledge, motivation, self-regulation, and mindframes (Zierer, 2014).

Feedback, evaluation, assessment, and rating

Grading plays a central role in most school systems around the world. Evaluating achievement – and thus the ability to accurately recognize errors – is an essential part of teaching.

For this reason, feedback and grading are closely related to each other, as teachers usually provide feedback in the form of grades. Student feedback is seen as an equivalent to evaluation, and is assumed that students grade teachers based on the mistakes that they make. This conceptual blur requires an explanation of what feedback means and what distinguishes it from evaluation, assessment, and ratings. In many cases, feedback fails in practice precisely because of an unclear definition of feedback. It is important to clarify the objectives of the individual concepts (see Table 3.1).

These definitions are of great importance for further discourse on this subject. Student feedback is highly controversial because it can be counterproductive and open the door to abuse, unless superiors are denied access to this feedback. Teachers must be sure that superiors can't use student feedback against them (which could have significant consequences for their career advancement).

Studies show that student feedback is very often used for evaluation and assessment purposes rather than as an opportunity for personal change (Elstad et al., 2017) and that instruments are used which do not do justice to the actual purpose (Kember et al., 2002). Under these conditions, students believe that their feedback to teachers does not change anything in the classroom (Spencer & Schmelkin, 2002; Chen & Hoshower, 2003), and teachers see student feedback as a controlling tool (Newton, 2000; Harvey, 2002).

Feedback as a motor for the development of instructional quality

Often at the end of a lesson, it can be observed that teachers want to stick to their plans and quickly finish what they have set out to do. The

TABLE 3.1 Definitions of key concepts

Feedback	Data-based exchange of information between people aimed at development and serving to adapt one's own behavior in response to feedback from others.
Evaluation	Investigation of whether and to what extent a behavior is suitable for achieving a desired target state or fulfilling a purpose.
Assessment	Verification of the extent to which a person's behavior or qualities are consistent with the evaluators' standards, usually expressed in terms of statements such as "good" or "bad."
Rating	Measures of personal characteristics, performance, and social behavior, usually expressed in terms of predicates, e.g., in the form of grades.

goal is to fulfill one's own plan in order to be able to say "I've gotten through this." This focus is problematic: On one hand, it leads away from the learners and in the direction of formal and structural specifications – all curriculum goals must be achieved. On the other hand, because of the hectic attempt to cram everything in at the end of the lesson, students are presented with new content in a short time and do not get a chance to review and practice – and often the very important consolidation of the lesson's content is left out. In view of the numerous research results, teachers are called upon to focus attention on student learning by calling on them to make visible what they have learned in the last few minutes, rather than spending time on a less productive teaching process. The point is not to do more but to do something else.

Procedures that question learners consciously and directly about the core components of teaching provide further opportunities for teachers to improve the quality of their instruction. A lesson's core components can be clarified with the help of the didactic hexagon (Figure 3.3).

Goals, content, methods, media, space, and time – these are the factors that decide whether teaching is successful and learning happens. In this respect, it is worth asking learners for feedback on these aspects and then reflecting on what happened during a lesson. Eliciting this kind of feedback requires courage, because teachers are not prepared for it – teacher training still sometimes socializes teachers to be "lone wolves" and to avoid mistakes at all stages, especially in lessons that are visited by superiors. Throughout their lives teachers are confronted with slogans such as "Teachers are right in the morning and wrong in the afternoon." But do have courage! Empirical research and the critical average effect size value of 0.4 show that a lot of teachers are already doing a lot right.

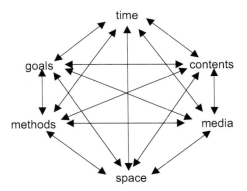

FIGURE 3.3 Didactic hexagon

Student feedback serves the purpose of improving instructional quality. It must be distinguished from evaluation, assessment, and ratings. Student feedback has a demonstrably positive effect not only on student achievement but also on the satisfaction and health of teachers. There is no scientific confirmation whatsoever that it has any negative impact on pedagogical practice. However, it takes courage to start asking for student feedback.

Bibliography

Aleamoni, L. M. (1999). Student rating myths versus research facts from 1924 to 1998. *Journal of Personnel Evaluation in Education*, 13(2), 153–166.

Brenner, P. J. (2009). *Wie Schule funktioniert. Schüler Lehrer, Eltern im Lernprozess.* Stuttgart: Kohlhammer.

Bromme, R., & Haag, L. (2004). Forschung zur Lehrerpersönlichkeit. In W. Helsper & J. Böhme (Hrsg.), *Handbuch der Schulforschung.* Wiesbaden: VS Verlag, S. 777–794.

Chen, Y., & Hoshower, L. B. (2003). Student evaluation of teaching effectiveness: An assessment of student perception and motivation. *Assessment & Evaluation in Higher Education*, 28(1), 71–88.

Ditton, H., & Arnoldt, B. (2004). Wirksamkeit von Schülerfeedback zum Fachunterricht. In J. Doll (Hrsg.), *Bildungsqualität von Schule.* Münster: Waxmann, S. 152–170.

Elstad, E., Lejonberg, E., & Christophersen, K. A. (2017). Student evaluation of high-school teaching: Which factors are associated with teachers' perception of the usefulness of being evaluated? *Journal for Educational Research Online*, 9(1), 99–117.

Enns, E., Rüegg, R., Schindler, B., & Strahm, P. (2002). *Lehren und Lernen im Tandem. Porträt eines partnerschaftlichen Fortbildungssystems.* Zentralstelle für Lehrerinnen und Lehrerfortbildung Kanton Bern.

Feldman, K. A. (2007). Identifying exemplary teachers and teaching: Evidence from student ratings. In *The scholarship of teaching and learning in higher education: An evidence-based perspective.* Dordrecht, The Netherlands: Springer, 93–143.

Harvey, L. (2002). The end of quality? *Quality in Higher Education*, 8(1), 5–22.

Hattie, J. (2008). *Visible Learning: A synthesis of over 800 meta-analyses relating to achievement.* London: Routledge.

Hattie, J., & Timperley, H. (2007). The power of feedback. *Review of Educational Research*, 77(1), 81–112.

Helmke, A., & Schrader, F. W. (2013). *EMU: Evidenzbasierte Methoden der Unterrichtsdiagnostik und -entwicklung.* Online: www.unterrichtsdiagnostik.de

Irving, S. E. (2004). *The Northern territory and validation of a student evaluation instrument to identify highly accomplished mathematics teachers* (Dissertation paper, Research Space, Auckland).

Kember, D., Leung, D.Y., & Kwan, K. (2002). Does the use of student feedback questionnaires improve the overall quality of teaching? *Assessment & Evaluation in Higher Education*, 27(5), 411–425.

Lenske, G. (2016). *Schülerfeedback in der Grundschule: Untersuchung zur Validität.* Münster: Waxmann.

Luft, J., & Ingram, H. (1955). *The Johari Window model.* Los Angeles: University of California Press.

Newton, J. (2000). Feeding the beast or improving quality? Academics' perceptions of quality assurance and quality monitoring. *Quality in Higher Education*, 6(2), 153–163.

Peterson, K. D. (2000). *Teacher evaluation: A comprehensive guide to new directions and practices.* Thousand Oaks: Corwin Press.

Peterson, K. D. (2004). Research on school teacher evaluation. *NASSP Bulletin*, 88(639), 60–79.

Spencer, K. J., & Schmelkin, L. P. (2002). Student perspectives on teaching and its evaluation. *Assessment & Evaluation in Higher Education*, 27(5), 397–409.

Zempel, J., & Moser, K. (2005). Feedback als Moderator der Validität von Selbstbeurteilungen. *Zeitschrift für Personalpsychologie*, 4(1), 19–27.

Zierer, K. (2014). *Hattie für gestresste Lehrer. Kernbotschaften und Handlungsempfehlungen aus John Hatties "Visible Learning" und "Visible Learning for Teachers".* Baltmannsweiler: Schneider Hohengehren.

CHAPTER

4

Student feedback in practice

Consider when, by whom, and how you have received feedback on your teaching. When was feedback helpful to you, and when was it not? What are the factors that make it difficult to obtain feedback?

This chapter attempts to shed light on student feedback from a practical teaching perspective. The individual phases of feedback are presented step-by-step. We show how feedback can be used from the perspectives of the recipient and the provider of feedback in a way that it leads to real benefits.

After reading this chapter, you should

- know different ways of implementing student feedback;
- have knowledge of high-quality criteria from different survey methods;
- be able to apply feedback management strategies as a feedback recipient;
- know how to conduct conversations about feedback;
- know the many possible applications of student feedback in practice;
- be able to implement a structured approach to making changes on the basis of feedback; and
- know the support systems available to teachers when implementing change processes.

Functions of student feedback

In contrast to evaluation, assessment, and ratings, which always serve the purpose of allocation or selection (e.g., promotion, access to functional positions, etc.) for teachers as well as students, feedback has the goal of personal development.

Essential functions of student feedback are:

- encouragement and motivation (from positive feedback);
- identification of personal strengths and weaknesses;
- prompts for reflection;
- identification of blind spots;
- democratization; and
- putting individual opinions in perspective (by anonymous surveys with the entire class or learning group).

As a teacher, how do I get helpful feedback on my teaching? First, ask yourself what you want from this feedback:

- What do you want to know?
- What do you not want to know?
- Do you want to test a specific hypothesis or obtain more general information?
- When and how often do you want to get feedback?
- When can you discuss the feedback received with the feedback providers?
- What experience do the feedback providers have with giving feedback?

Generally speaking, student feedback can cover two areas of content: student achievement and teaching as a process.

Obtaining feedback through achievement results

The first category of feedback is aimed at finding out whether and to what extent student achievement can be improved. In the following, we present three examples of how to make learning visible at the end of a lesson (cf. Hattie & Zierer, 2017) and help you develop your own ideas that you can discuss with your colleagues.

Student feedback in practice

The first example is a math lesson in which the students have worked out the formulas for sine and cosine – embedded in the teaching sequence "What is the significance of longitude and latitude?" The teacher develops the synthesis, shown in Figure 4.1, at the blackboard.

The students transfer this information to their notebooks, which not only serves the purpose of activation but is also a first and important form of consolidation and repetition. This activity can be followed by further exercises with the formulas, before all exercise books are closed at the end of the lesson and the students are asked to complete the task illustrated in Figure 4.2.

What is the significance of longitude and latitude? The sine and cosine function

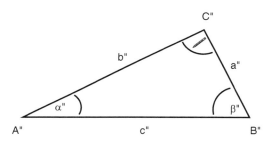
FIGURE 4.1 Task example

$$\sin\alpha = \frac{opposite\ leg}{hypothenuse} = \frac{a}{c}$$

$$\cos\alpha = \frac{adjacent\ leg}{hypothenuse} = \frac{b}{c}$$

The sine and cosine function

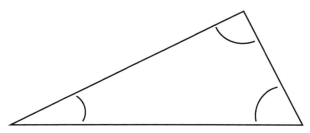
FIGURE 4.2 Task example

$sin\alpha = \underline{} = \underline{}$

$cos\alpha = \underline{} = \underline{}$

1						N	O	R	W	A	Y		M	A	P	L	E	
2										L	I	M	E		T	R	E	E
3								A	L	D	E	R						
4								A	C	O	R	N						
5										O	A	K		T	R	E	E	
6							B	I	R	C	H							
7							H	O	R	N	B	E	A	M				
8							C	H	E	S	T	N	U	T				
9						B	E	E	C	H								
10			W	A	L	N	U	T										

FIGURE 4.3 Task example

This task can be assigned to the area of reproduction – an important requirement for introductory lessons, especially since a deep understanding (transfer and problem solving) is based on a reliable understanding of the surface (reproduction and reorganization).

The second example is a quiz, which will help students to quickly test their knowledge of important terms. This procedure is a simple form of a reorganization task. At the end of a lesson in which different deciduous trees were dealt with on the basis of their leaves and fruits, the following worksheet can be used to make achievement visible. The numbers 1 to 12 can be replaced by pictures of leaves and fruits, supplemented by appropriate texts, or extended by a suitable description, which the teacher reads out (Figure 4.3).

As a third example, an open question is formulated with the aim of making in-depth understanding visible. The task was preceded by lessons in which Picasso and his works of art were the subject of discussion (cf. Hattie, 2013):

Student feedback in practice

What did Picasso want to express with the painting *Guernica*? Give reasons for your opinion.

_____

_____

_____

_____

FIGURE 4.4 Task example

The three examples presented show that it is possible for teachers to gain information on how students learn without too much effort. Essentially, the aim is to ask about the impact of the teaching process on the learning process and to look for evidence that makes the connection between the two processes visible. It is crucial for the teacher to succeed in not only collecting the data but also reflecting on and using it for teaching.

In addition to these methods, achievement testing is one of the central tasks of teachers in many countries. In this respect, the following suggestions (Figure 4.5) point out aspects that can help to make testing a means of checking the effectiveness of teachers' own thinking and actions – to make the learning of children and young people visible and to promote the development of teaching (cf. Hattie & Zierer, 2017).

First, weighting by task type: It is helpful to divide the tasks into the areas of reproduction, reorganization, transfer, and problem solving. By specifying these areas, it is possible to make differentiated statements about the learners and the lessons. This can be of interest with regard to both the performance of an individual student and the average grade within a class. Two examples: Student 10, "Jacob," scored 9 out of 28 points and Student 13, "Maria," scored 10 out of 28 points. Both seem to have performed equally well. However, a closer look at the scores for the task types reveals the following: While Student 10 scored the most points in transfer and problem solving, Student 13 scored almost exclusively in reproduction and reorganization. The conclusions to be drawn from this that the learning and working methods of Student 10 require support, whereas Student 13 is rather deficient with regard to the subject-specific prerequisites. These findings can be discussed with the students. If the conclusions are confirmed, that in the following lessons, changes should be made accordingly: In the case of Student 10, for example, it would be more important than in the past to check his homework, to pay attention to proper exercise book entries, and to introduce individual strategies for memorization. In the case of Student 13, her reading skills could be improved in collaboration with

Student feedback in practice

Test result sheet

Grade	9
Date	2016-04-16
Subject	Maths

weight	task 1	task 2	task 3	task 4	task 5	task 6	task 7	task 8		tatal	reccomendation
reproduction	6					4		4		14	40%
reorganization			4				4			8	30%
transfer		2		2						4	20%
problem-solving					2					2	10%
									total score	28	100%

	task 1	task 2	task 3	task 4	task 5	task 6	task 7	task 8			
numbers and calculations	6							4		10	36
factual mathematics		2	4		2		4			12	43
geometry				2		4				6	21

		task 1	task 2	task 3	task 4	task 5	task 6	task 7	task 8	task 9	task 10	total	grade
1	Andrew	6	3	4	2	2	1	4	1			23	B
2	Benjamin	6	2	4	2	2	4	4	4			28	A
3	Charlotte	6	2	4	2	2	2	4	4			26	A
4	Daniel	5	1	3	0	3	0	3	2			17	D
5	Eric	4	1	2	0	3	0	4	3			17	D
6	Erederic	6	2	4	2	1	3	2	0			20	C
7	Gary	6	2	3	0	2	3	4	0			20	C
8	Henry	6	2	3	0	2	1	4	0			18	D
9	Isabella	6	0	4	2	2	4	4	4			26	A
10	Jacob	0	2	1	2	2	1	1	0			9	F
11	Karen	6	2	3	2	2	3	4	2			24	B
12	Luke	3	1	3	2	2	4	4	4			23	B
13	Maria	6	0	0	0	0	0	0	4			10	F
14	Nadia	6	2	4	2	2	4	2	0			22	C
15	Ortis	6	2	4	2	2	4	4	4			28	A
16	Paula	6	2	4	2	1	4	4	2			25	B
17	Rebecca	6	2	4	2	2	4	4	4			28	A
18	Sophia	6	0	3	1	2	3	1	4			20	C
19	Ted	6	2	2	1	3	4	0	0			18	D
20	Umberto	6	0	3	0	0	2	4	0			15	F
21	Veronica	6	2	4	1	2	4	4	4			27	D
22	Wendy	6	1	3	2	0	4	4	0			20	C
23	Zach	6	2	4	2	2	4	4	4			28	A
	percentual average	91,3%	76,1%	79,3%	67,4%	89,1%	68,5%	79,3%	54,3%			76,4%	

distribution of grades

Grading key	from	to	credits
A	100%	90%	25
B	89%	80%	22
C	79%	70%	20
D	69%	60%	17
F	59%	0	0

FIGURE 4.5 Test result sheet

parents through daily reading and writing tasks on topics from her life, and creative and flexible thinking could be initiated through an increasing variation of the practice phases.

Second, information on task difficulty by means of average performance: It is also helpful to calculate the average score of each task, which should not be less than 20%. If this value is not reached, this is an indication that something has gone wrong in class and that the task was too difficult for the students. Depending on the type of task and its difficulty, it is therefore possible to determine the effectiveness of teaching or the overall achievement level and the learning and methods of the students. The average of 5.5 points (92.0%) on Task 1 in Figure 4.5 suggests that the learners mastered this reproductive task very well, which allows conclusions to be drawn either on the teaching or on the students' learning performance. In Task 8, however, where on average only 2.1 out of 4 points (53.3%) of reproductive performance was achieved, corresponding shortcomings can be assumed. With regard to the subsequent lessons, it is therefore necessary to call into question the choice of objectives and content in connection with the use of methods and media.

Third, the distribution of grades: The distribution of grades and the grading key are important sources of information. Empirical studies indicate that a criterion-oriented reference standard should be preferred to a socially oriented one, if possible coupled with a student-oriented one. This last reference standard can be considered especially in the form of a differentiated commentary at the end of a school assignment containing positive statements on the learning process and self-regulation. Regarding a criterion-oriented reference standard and the definition of the grading key, it is difficult to make a "general recommendation," since they depend greatly on individual and situational factors and are often guided by intuitive assessments. We therefore propose the following procedure, which takes into account the mentioned scientific guidelines and testing theory mentioned earlier but places pragmatics at the center of attention: Determine the distribution of points according to the types of tasks and their importance for teaching and for each school task. The higher the total score, the smaller the measurement error and the greater the reliability of the assessment. A similar approach is recommended for the grading key, which is created on the basis of a minimum competence (Grade D): Partially linear scales (as in Figure 4.3) have proven helpful in practice, whereas linear and non-linear scales lead to various problems (fixed minimum competence on the one hand and increased measurement errors on the other). In both cases, the lessons held must be the basis for both, meaning that minor deviations are possible and necessary on a case-by-case basis. In addition, the criteria for success (criterion-oriented reference standard) should be made known to the students in advance. This allows a fair and relatively objective procedure.

But what should one do if the results of a test are too good or too bad? Actually, the first test results that are "too good" do not cause real problems: Isn't it the goal of all educational efforts to make sure that all children reach the intended goal? However, this issue arises again and again, especially in comparing individual classes or schools. In our opinion, a revision of the grading key to a statistical standard distribution or an "acceptable" average grade of C (socially oriented reference standard), seems inadmissible – especially since from a pedagogical point of view it is not justifiable for children to answer for their teacher's shortcomings or the fact that they are in a high-achieving class and are therefore being compared to a different standard. Weaker students would be the victims of such measures and could feel deceived if, after their last test, they had followed the advice of the teacher on their individual progress (student-oriented reference standard). In this case, the teacher in charge must think about whether the test was too easy and if necessary make the appropriate changes in their lessons. Preceding and subsequent lessons are linked to the planning and evaluation of tests. Both extremes make it clear how strongly the preceding and subsequent lessons are linked to the planning and evaluation of tests.

Asking students how they perceive teaching

In the examples shown so far, the aim was to make the achievement of students visible. The purpose of the second category of feedback is to provide teachers with information on how students have perceived their lessons.

The simplest means of eliciting feedback is to talk to students and ask them what they think about a lesson or how they assess their own benefit from this lesson. This requires little time and effort and can be carried out practically at the end of every lesson. In general, however, the results of such feedback involve the following disadvantages:

- They are very general and do not provide detailed information.
- They are determined by individuals and do not reflect the opinion of the whole class (shy and reserved students do not speak out).
- Fears of students that their feedback can lead to a personal disadvantage can prevent honest criticism.
- They do not open up clearly defined opportunities for change.

In order to be able to use student feedback in a more solution-oriented way, it makes sense to

- have clearly defined criteria;
- ask the whole class; and
- conduct surveys anonymously.

This can be done in different ways. For example, a simple impression can be achieved by means of a feedback coordinate system or a feedback target, in which students attach adhesive dots to a two-dimensional coordinate system after completing a learning unit. This can be done anonymously if the coordinate system is placed out of the teacher's sight while the students attach their dots. Two important aspects of teaching can be included: success of group work and knowledge acquisition (Figure 4.6).

For example, if on one hand a learner thinks that the group work has gone well and the knowledge gain is high, then he or she places a dot in the upper right corner. If, on the other hand, he or she believes that the group work did not go well and that the knowledge gain is low, he or she puts a dot in the lower left corner. It takes only a few minutes to put a poster with this feedback coordinate system on the classroom door and have students attach their dots as they leave. This feedback can be obtained quickly, but it can provide important information about the lesson.

This process can be developed further depending on the maturity of the students; there are plenty of additional ideas in the didactics literature. Here is another example, the feedback target (Figure 4.7).

As striking as the feedback target is at first glance, it unfortunately has some flaws: On the one hand, it suggests completeness, but this is not the case. Only a selection of aspects of the learning environment is mentioned in it. On the other hand, distortions caused by the shape of a circular section cannot be avoided: The closer the dots come to the center

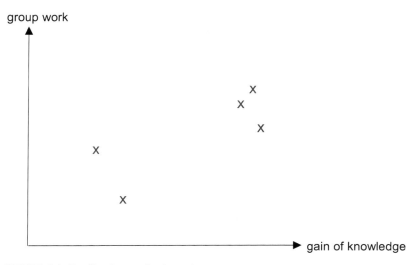

FIGURE 4.6 Feedback coordinate system

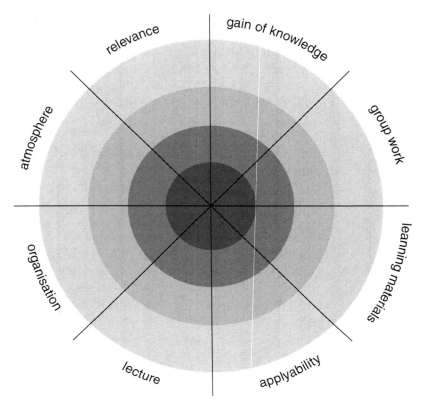

FIGURE 4.7 Feedback target

of the circle, the smaller the available space is and the lower the probability gets for the sector to be selected. And vice versa, the further the dots come to the edge of the circle, the larger the available space and the higher the probability to be selected. This is not really a serious disadvantage, but aspects like this have to be discussed with the students during the assignment and taken into consideration during the interpretation.

Similar feedback can be obtained easily with the help of bar charts (Figure 4.8). Here, again, the teacher gets an impression of how successful the lesson was according to subjective student perception and with regard to the chosen categories. For example, if students think that the atmosphere has been very positive for learning, a dot comes close to 100, and if they think that their gain of knowledge was low, they put the dot further down, for example at 50.

Questionnaires are the most helpful means of getting differentiated feedback about a lesson or a longer learning unit. They offer the

Student feedback in practice

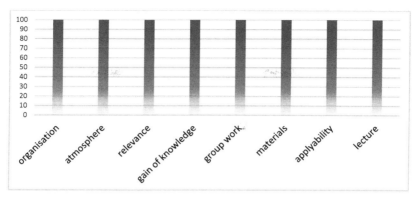

FIGURE 4.8 Feedback chart

advantages of high reliability, because they include information from an entire class instead of individual pupils.

Take Figure 4.9 as an example, the result of student feedback compared to a teacher's self-perception about the factor "challenge," and consider which conversations can and must follow. While the teacher answered most items in the category "challenge" with "I agree", students mostly disagreed or rather disagreed with these items.

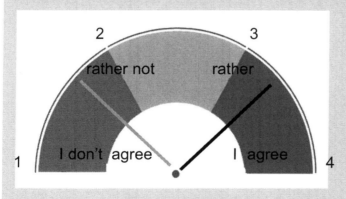

FIGURE 4.9 Self-perception and student feedback

Just find out what suits you best. There is no "golden path" of the correct methods. Checking what is helpful to you is the only recommendation that we can make: Evidence-based diversity of methods is key!

It has already been mentioned that how teachers deal with student feedback is a measure of expertise. The examples we cited clarify this. At first glance, students who use a feedback coordinate system or a feedback target give feedback only at the task and process level but no feedback at the level of self-regulation. Additionally, they provide feedback only from the perspective of the present. Nonetheless, the teacher can use this information to compare this perspective with a past perspective by placing earlier feedback next to it and using it to generate future-oriented feedback. Likewise, it can also become clear from a response at the task level what consequences this has for the future teaching process and the teacher's self-regulation. This shows that feedback is not something carved in stone. Feedback is the ticket to an infinite dialogue. Providing feedback implies receiving feedback and vice versa.

The feedback methods you been exposed to in this chapter and some others are summarized in Table 4.1, which provides an overview of the advantages and disadvantages.

Apart from the nature of and technical implementation of feedback, it is important to consider how to overcome your own concerns. Because feedback is not only a matter of competence but also – and above all – a question of mindframes, it is not uncommon for such concerns to play an important role. The following model, which distinguishes between three steps, helps you to get a grip on your concerns.

In order to make the first step, "door openers" can be used, that is, surveys on aspects that have nothing to do with the teacher (e.g., a questionnaire on the classroom climate). In a next step, questions can be asked on the basis of clearly defined criteria, which can be answered on a scale of "I don't agree," "I rather don't agree," "I rather agree," and "I agree." This feedback refers to behavior in a particular situation (e.g., a particular lesson) and focuses on the areas of process and self-regulation. One must decide on one's own whether to go to the third step to get feedback on one's own personal characteristics, for example using free-text items.

Asking the right questions

"I've used student feedback, but I didn't benefit from it." This is a sentence we often hear from teachers. This opinion is diametrically opposed to the empirical research findings described in Chapter 3.

TABLE 4.1 Feedback methods overview

METHODS	ADVANTAGES	DISADVANTAGES
Free feedback (oral, in conversation)	• low time expenditure • low preparatory effort	• dominated by individual opinions • low significance • low degree of differentiation • no anonymity
Feedback coordinate system or target	• low time expenditure • always feasible	• limited range of recorded aspects • earnings distortions
Questionnaire	• high expressiveness • high differentiation • high reliability due to the coverage of a larger group of respondents	• time expenditure
Free feedback (in writing and anonymously)	• important hints on blind spots possible • makes it possible to address specific issues in a precise and differentiated manner • enables suggestions and can lead directly to solutions	• risk of arbitrariness • danger of self-esteem endangering answers • risk of overvaluing individual opinions
Lesson summary by students	• information about learning success • additional backup of the hourly content	• limited to one or few learners
Achievement test	• information on the learning success of the entire learning group • information on how to continue planning lessons	• purely summative, therefore no information about the lessons themselves • associated with time for correction

Use the following item examples (for which students are supposed to indicate their agreement/disagreement) to consider how inappropriate items can affect the success of student feedback:

"The teacher can explain the material well."

"The teacher knows her/his subject well."

Student feedback in practice

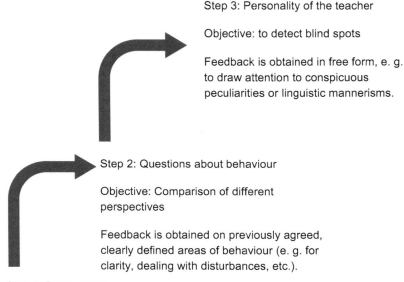

Step 3: Personality of the teacher

Objective: to detect blind spots

Feedback is obtained in free form, e. g. to draw attention to conspicuous peculiarities or linguistic mannerisms.

Step 2: Questions about behaviour

Objective: Comparison of different perspectives

Feedback is obtained on previously agreed, clearly defined areas of behaviour (e. g. for clarity, dealing with disturbances, etc.).

Step 1: Door opener

Objective: Become familiar with feedback

Feedback is collected on areas that have nothing to do with the teacher, e. g. on the class climate or collaboration during a group work.

FIGURE 4.10 Steps to obtain feedback from lessons

Source: Adapted from Strahm (2008).

"The teacher is fun sometimes."

"I am attentive in class and keep quiet."

"I enjoyed the lesson."

Search the internet for "methods of student feedback." You will find that this term calls up a hodgepodge of ideas and many techniques used for obtaining feedback. From the "feedback hand" to the "corner method," from the "traffic light prism" and "flash feedback" to "just write down what you liked and what you didn't like," you will encounter a vast pool of simple ad-hoc methods. A closer look reveals that these methods provide completely different kinds of information. Consequently, it is obvious that not every form of feedback can provide the same benefits for learners and teachers.

When feedback is given to teachers by learners on the basis of their subjective experience, the purpose is to answer the following questions:

- How do students perceive teaching?
- To what extent is the way of teaching suitable for initiating successful learning processes?
- Where are obstacles to student learning?
- How can these obstacles be mastered by teachers and students together?

Ad-hoc methods, like those outlined earlier (Table 4.1), can be used in meaningful ways to address these questions and initiate a dialogue between students and teachers. In this respect, they have their justification and significance. However, all these methods also have their limitations. We would now like to take a small excursion, explaining the concepts of objectivity, reliability, and validity.

Objectivity

The methods mentioned in this chapter (Table 4.1) have low objectivity, as the results depend on the respondent, that is, the teacher. The teacher influences the students' response behavior both through verbal and non-verbal aspects of the way of asking and through immediate reactions.

Reliability

The methods have a low reliability because not all learners are asked to provide information at the same time. In this way, individual opinions are overestimated and the opinion of shy and reserved students is overlooked.

Validity

Finally, the methods mentioned have a low validity: The results obtained in these ways are superimposed to a large extent by social interaction processes. Response distortions occur due to two major sources of error. A lack of anonymity leads to effects of social desirability, which are particularly increased by the fact that there is a hierarchical divide between feedback recipients and feedback providers and that the latter have to fear negative consequences in the case of critical feedback (Schnell et al., 2005). For example, if a teacher asks the class for spontaneous feedback on how the lesson was perceived, negative feedback due to fear of penalties from the teacher (e.g., a bad grade) or positive feedback due to fear of penalties by the group (e.g., "teacher's pet!") can be withheld.

In addition, the response behavior of individual feedback providers in non-anonymous response situations depends greatly on the response behavior of the other feedback providers. So-called conformity effects result from the fact that, especially in case of uncertainty regarding a suitable answer, the response of other group members is imitated – a long known phenomenon from social psychology (Latane, 1981). If, for example, students are to give feedback on an aspect of the lesson in the form of a one-sentence flash response, the feedback providers are likely to adapt to the answers given by the students before them. If these are positive, the probability that a negative aspect will be addressed decreases with every subsequent answer and vice versa.

The aforementioned ad-hoc methods bear the risk of making the dialogue about feedback more difficult, possibly even impossible, providing only a reduced type of information. The core of obtaining student feedback, however, is for teachers to use the students' point of view to reflect on their own behavior.

Student feedback and the quality of teaching

Can students really give valid feedback on the quality of teaching? The common mistrust in students' diagnostic capabilities in terms of the quality of teaching is unfounded in several respects: Even students at primary level can assess the basic dimensions of teaching quality (Lenske, 2016). Furthermore, averaged student feedback data are reliable and correspond to the findings of instructional research (Gruehn, 2000).

The most interesting finding of the research carried out so far, however, is that students' feedback on the quality of teaching very precisely predicts the objectively measurable results. Various studies and reviews indicate a positive correlation between student feedback for a particular teacher and the actual achievement or increase in competence caused by this teacher (Braun & Leidner, 2009; Onwuegbuzie et al., 2009; Balch, 2012). A group of researchers from the Gates Foundation (2013) showed that student feedback about the quality of teaching is highly correlated with the actual outcomes of teaching. Value-added scores that reflect teachers' contributions to their students' achievement independently of other influencing variables are clearly linked to student feedback on seven central characteristics of teaching quality. This correlation is illustrated in Figure 4.11 for mathematics.

The actual increase in the achievement of students of the 25% teachers who received the most favorable feedback in the Tripod 7C questionnaire was about 0.05 points higher than the actual increase in the number of students of the 25% teachers who received the most unfavorable feedback in the same questionnaire. This difference corresponds to an advantage in achievement of about 4 1/2 months. In other words, student feedback can predict learning outcomes with extreme precision if an empirically convincing model of teaching quality and a suitable measuring instrument are used.

Criteria-based questionnaires

A major advantage of questionnaires over other instruments or methods is that they make results visible on the basis of predefined criteria. Thus, the focus shifts from a primarily subjective response, which involves the risk of dealing with topics concerning their sense of self-worth, to a standardized response, taking into account scientifically based quality features. Put more simply, it is not about who a teacher is but about what a teacher does in a concrete situation, in a concrete class, and in a concrete subject.

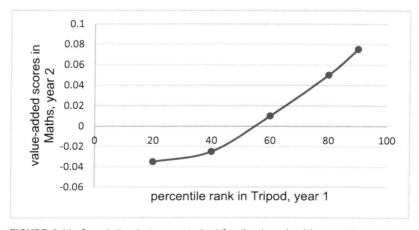

FIGURE 4.11 Correlation between student feedback and achievement
Source: Gates Foundation (2013, p. 10).

Focusing on teaching quality features is an important step towards eliciting effective feedback. But caution is necessary: For feedback to be effective, the question of which criteria are used is vital. Teachers have different ideas about "good teaching" due to their personal experience. It has become common for school principals to have their teachers develop feedback questionnaires based on their personal experience – sometimes during one-afternoon sessions. How could teachers be able to develop a meaningful questionnaire in such a short time when this task takes research groups months or years? A look at the following examples (items that are taken from "self-made" questionnaires, along with our commentary) shows why the development of feedback questionnaires takes time and expertise:

Example 1: "The teacher can explain the material well." (Do you agree, rather agree, rather disagree, or disagree?)

The response to this item requires a normative judgment. Inadequate operationalization of what "well" actually means prevents the teacher from gaining any useful information. The biggest problem, however, is that the teacher cannot draw any conclusions from answers to this item as to *why* her or his way of explaining material was perceived as good or less good. If the feedback is to be used to make behavioral changes (if necessary), this item does not provide an opportunity to do so, because it does not describe behavior but rather a relatively stable characteristic of the person, namely his or her explanatory competence. In the end, the person is evaluated (level of the task) and no opportunity of change is opened (level of self-regulation).

Example 2: "The teacher knows her/his subject well." (Do you agree, rather agree, rather disagree, or disagree?)

As in Example 1, this item refers to a relatively stable characteristic of the person (subject matter knowledge) and additionally requires students to assess this knowledge, which they are usually unable to do. Thus, the item provides unreliable information. In this way, this feedback is highly likely to run the risk of not stimulating any constructive reflective processes but can even threaten the teacher's self-esteem if the response is unfavorable. At the same time, it does not offer any solution for possible change.

Student feedback in practice

Example 3: "The teacher is fun sometimes." (Do you agree, rather agree, rather disagree, or disagree?)

The restriction by the operator "sometimes" leads to an inaccuracy of the item. The formulation produces a phenomenon called *acquiescence* (Moosbrugger & Kelava, 2007). This means that you tend to agree with the item regardless of its content. How many people would you spontaneously think of whom you would call "fun?" In the case that this item was answered on a discrete scale from "always correct" to "never correct," the item statement and its response format would be contradictory due to the addition of "sometimes": A behavior cannot be shown "always" and "sometimes" at the same time. And finally, the question remains: What does the fact that someone is "fun" have to do with the quality of teaching?

Example 4: "The teacher helps me be attentive and makes me keep quiet." (Do you agree, rather agree, rather disagree, or disagree?)

The item contains a double statement. The two individual statements "The teacher helps me be attentive" and "makes me keep quiet" can sometimes be answered very differently by students. The item provokes response distortions by combining two statements that are independent of each other and can be perceived in completely different ways.

Item example 5: "I enjoyed the lesson." (Do you agree, rather agree, rather disagree, or disagree?)

This item is a "classic" item – on the one hand because it is found in many questionnaires used in schools; on the other hand because it is often used in test theory lectures as an example of a bad item. The item does not provide any information about the quality of teaching. Students may have enjoyed themselves for a variety of reasons, even reasons that have nothing to do with teaching or learning. Since there is no relation between the item statement and the intention of the feedback recipient, that is, reflection on one's own instructional behavior, the interpretation of the results is highly arbitrary.

On the basis of these five item examples, we attempted to clarify that a questionnaire cannot simply be created in an ad-hoc way. Consequently, it is not only important whether feedback is based on criteria but also *what criteria* are used. "Self-made" questionnaires can of course provide valuable insights under certain conditions, but they have undeniable limitations.

Evidence-based questionnaires

In contrast to ad-hoc instruments, evidence-based questionnaires (cf. Wisniewski & Zierer, 2017a) are helpful for obtaining well-founded feedback on teaching. They contain items that do not reflect the subjective theories of individual teachers but whose relatedness to achievement or other criteria can be validated by scientific studies.

Validated questionnaires

Instruments such as Tripod's 7C (Gates Foundation, 2012) or teaCh (Wisniewski & Zierer, available at www.visiblefeedback.com) go one step further than evidence-based questionnaires in that they have been validated on the basis of extensive samples. In this respect, not only is the content of the items supported by scientific evidence, but also the items have also been examined with the help of statistical methods. These instruments may be represent the gold standard, not only from the perspective of educational science but also from the perspective of teaching practice. They meet the highest quality standards and consequently establish profound opportunities for conversation about teaching.

It is obvious that teachers do not have to be researchers but evaluators. The former would be asking too much of teachers, because the development of questionnaires requires special knowledge and takes a lot of time. However, being an evaluator is a core element of the profession. It makes sense for teachers to use the best questionnaires available. Nevertheless, it is also necessary for an evaluator to be cautious: Not everything that is offered on the internet, for example, meets scientific criteria! For several years now, teachers have been using a variety of tools to obtain feedback from students. The quality of these instruments varies considerably. At the end of the day, the quality of the instrument determines whether there is a real information gain and whether feedback can be used for a dialogue about teaching and learning.

Table 4.2 gives an overview of the three types of questionnaires that can be used to obtain classroom feedback.

TABLE 4.2 Types of questionnaires for classroom feedback

TYPE	FOUNDATION
ad-hoc instruments	none or purely subjective experience and subjective theories
evidence-based instruments	empirically measurable correlations of items with objective criteria like achievement
validated, evidence-based instruments (gold standard)	empirically measurable correlations of items with objective criteria like achievement and statistically provable quality criteria

Earlier in this chapter, we tried to show what feedback items should *not* look like. This leads to the question of what good questionnaires look like. The 7Cs developed in the MET project (2010) are convincing and recommendable. The 7Cs questionnaire contains the following categories of instructional quality.

7Cs

- Challenge (expectations of performance; encouragement of effort, endurance, and persistence)
- Control (efficient classroom management, active use of time, establishment of rules and procedures)
- Care (emotional care and support, encouragement)
- Confer (promoting and granting student participation; accepting student feedback)
- Captivate (developing and maintaining a fascination for the subject)
- Clarify (structuring; transparency; multiple explanations and approaches)
- Consolidate (consolidation; summary; confirmation)

The careful construction of a questionnaire that is in accordance with the principles of measurement theory as well as demands of practitioners requires a considerable amount of effort. This may be illustrated by the example of the teaCh questionnaire (Wisniewski & Zierer, in prep.) on www.visiblefeedback.com (Figure 4.12). This questionnaire was developed in four steps with the aim of providing teachers with meaningful and usable student

Student feedback in practice

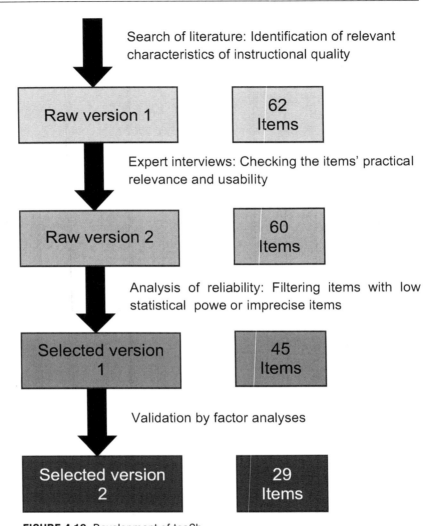

FIGURE 4.12 Development of teaCh

feedback about their teaching. The research resulted in a factorial structure that supports the 7Cs. In other words, this model seems to be very well suited to describe the general quality of teaching in a valid way.

Each item of teaCh is based on at least two studies or one meta-analysis and has been tested for its practicability by several experts, including teachers, school administrators, teacher trainers, and students.

Following are two examples of how this scientific derivation has taken place.

Example 1: The teacher created an undisturbed learning atmosphere.
Scientific relevance:

The management of groups plays an important role in the teaching process. Effective classroom management is a classroom variable that is highly and consistently linked to achievement. While teachers who take preventive action against classroom disturbances spend only 1 to 3% of their teaching time on disciplinary measures, those who mainly react to disturbances spend between 7 and 18.5% of their teaching time on such measures. This means that in the case of a twelve-year schooling period, there is a difference of about two years in teaching time.

(Bennett & Smilanich, 1994)

Example 2: The teacher talked to me in an appreciative way.
Scientific relevance:

Successful teachers build positive and appreciative relationships with their students. Teachers are only accepted by students as leaders if they build "an appreciative, respectful and caring relationship."

(Schönbächler, 2008, p. 66)

The questionnaire was subjected to an item analysis (statistical power, internal consistency, homogeneity) on the basis of a sample of more than 1,000 data sets and validated on the basis exploratory and confirmatory factor analyses (see Wisniewski & Zierer, in preparation). The evaluation determined whether the answers of the sample statistically support or derive from the underlying model of teaching quality and consequently whether the instrument really measures what it is supposed to measure.

Figure 4.13 shows the structural model of the teaCh questionnaire for readers interested in designing a questionnaire. The statistical examination revealed seven categories that correspond to the 7Cs of the MET project. The 27 individual items "load" with certain values on these categories, which is indicated by arrows from the categories to the individual items. These values should be as high as possible for a good model (greater than 0.5).

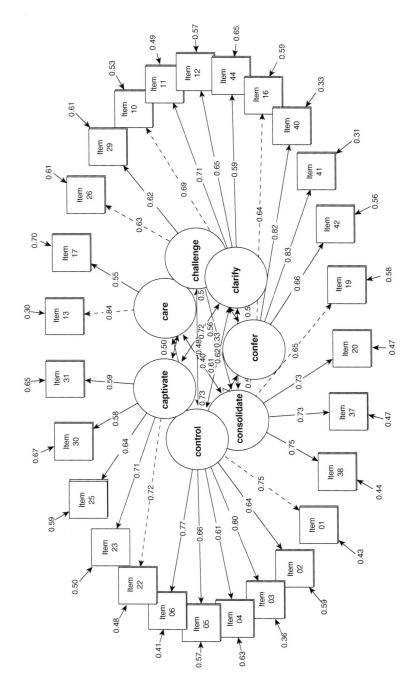

FIGURE 4.13 Structural model of teaCh

Talking about feedback (as recipient)

Feedback providers want to know what happens after they provide their feedback. An essential part of any feedback is therefore the subsequent focus. In the case of student feedback, this takes place as a classroom debriefing in the next lesson. If students discover that they are supposed to give feedback, but this remains without consequence, they no longer recognize any benefit and will not take part in further surveys with a serious attitude or will no longer participate at all.

The following questions can be discussed during the debriefing (it is not an exhaustive list of suggestions):

- Which factors contributed to the success of the students?
- Which factors hindered the success of the students' learning?
- Which criteria for a successful lesson were strong?
- Which criteria for a successful lesson were weak?
- Which criteria do feedback recipients and feedback providers perceive differently?

At the end of every debriefing, there are concrete target agreements. These can be manifold. Here are just a few examples to illustrate:

- "When you are working in groups, I will make sure that it's clear what each individual has to do."
- "I will pay more attention to including all students when we work on difficult tasks."
- "I will be less grumpy on Monday mornings."

In order to check whether the changes have been effective, it is possible to carry out a new survey after a few weeks.

Talking about feedback (as provider)

Up to now, we have dealt with feedback from the perspective of the recipient. In the following, we will discuss the other perspective, that of the feedback provider. When student feedback is accompanied by collegial visitation or peer mentoring, teachers have to be able to discuss feedback and sometimes provide their own feedback.

Student feedback in practice

Compare the following two examples of feedback on a colleague's teaching and see which one you find more helpful. Try to identify the reasons for this as accurately as possible.

This was actually a great lesson! You're really good at explaining things, but if I were you, I'd be more careful to ensure that there really is silence while you are explaining something. I would have done the transitions between the different parts of the lesson differently. You should make sure somehow that's a little more "fluid." You could have called on the students sitting in the back much more often! They're quite a bother. I also have a few of them in my class and I keep calling on them so they don't get any ideas. In general, one should be more careful that a little more discipline prevails. Maybe you're a little too good-natured.	The students were attentive and contributed a lot of good things to the lesson. It became very clear to everyone what the goal of the lesson was. Your explanations were also easy to understand. I found the relationship between you and your class to be relaxed and respectful. This has certainly contributed to the success of the lesson. But I noticed that it was rather noisy at several times, especially in the back rows. On the one hand, I attribute this to the fact that the transitions between the teaching phases were somewhat abrupt and, on the other hand, to the fact that a few students couldn't follow. Try inserting short repetitions between the phases and calling on the students in the back row more often.

The examples show two different ways of giving someone feedback. In principle, helpful feedback can be distinguished from unhelpful feedback on the basis of the criteria in Table 4.3.

Criteria for successful feedback

Most teachers are familiar with "should have, could have, might have" feedback. In debriefings of lessons (whether with head teachers, teacher trainers, or colleagues), feedback providers often formulate numerous statements about what could or should have been done differently in one place or another, sometimes down to the smallest detail: "At this point students could have been involved even more, and in this part you could have used a silent impulse instead of a question," etc. As typical as this type of feedback is, it is also more than problematic. It is a central result of research that feedback is perceived to be of little help when it is unstructured and ambiguous, contains numerous pieces of advice of a general nature, and ignores the feedback recipient's own views and possible solutions (Frommer & Bovet,

Student feedback in practice

TABLE 4.3 Criteria for successful feedback

CRITERIA FOR SUCCESSFUL FEEDBACK	CRITERIA FOR LESS SUCCESSFUL FEEDBACK
more descriptive, observant	more assessing, judging, interpreting
more concrete	more general
more requested	more forced
more inviting	more rebuking
more behavior-related	more character-related
more immediate and situational	more delayed
more clear and precise	more vague
more verifiable by third parties	more restricted to dynamic situations

Source: See Strahm (2008).

1999). Conversations like this can easily lead to frustration and lost opportunities for behavioral change.

The following example illustrates a class debriefing after student feedback was received:

A teacher interviewed ninth-grade students on six items about motivation, asking them to agree, rather agree, rather disagree, or disagree to these items:

1 The requirement level of the lesson was appropriate for me.

2 The pace of the lesson was appropriate for me.

3 The teacher used the lesson time in such a way that I was able to make progress.

4 The teacher has helped me to recognize connections myself.

5 The contents of the lesson were taught by the teacher in an interesting way.

6 The teacher varied different teaching methods.

As Figure 4.14 shows, the teacher perceived the degree of motivation in all areas as very high. For items three to six, the students largely agreed with this assessment. On the other hand, they agreed to items one and two less than their teacher did.

A lot about captivating students works very well in this class. The deviating perceptions of the first two items can be used as a basis for discussion.

■ Why were the level of difficulty and pace of the lesson not appropriate for the learners?

■ What measures can be taken to achieve a better fit?

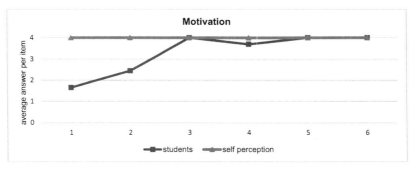

1: I don't agree • 2: I rather don't agree • 3: I rather agree • 4: I agree • 0: no answer

FIGURE 4.14 Feedback on six items from the "Captivate" category

Discussing the lesson on the basis of the collected data ensures that clear and verifiable change targets can be defined. The differentiated mapping of the "motivation" area using six empirically verified items also makes it possible to clearly identify the direction in which a possible change can take place.

The success of feedback also depends on how it is communicated. If it is communicated clearly, it generates high satisfaction and acceptance in the feedback recipient and leads to an intention to change his or her behavior if necessary. From an empirical point of view, the following points can be demonstrated (Kanning & Rustige, 2012): Satisfaction and acceptance depend to a large extent on the quality of the feedback, that is, on how substantively and comprehensibly it explains why something was perceived as positive or negative. If suggestions are made as to what should be changed, it is crucial to substantiate this arguably soundly ("I am your teacher trainer," by the way, is not such a sound underpinning). Instead of "should have, could have, might have" feedback, a structured procedure including the following steps is preferable:

1 comparison of the perspectives of the feedback recipient and the feedback provider with regard to concrete quality criteria;
2 thematization of the congruence and discrepancies between feedback and self-perception and the reasons for them;
3 joint consideration of possibilities for improvement based on the discrepancies; and
4 agreement on goal(s).

Student feedback in practice

For the process of debriefing, Lorenz (2014) states that feedback should be

- subjective;
- specific;
- descriptive;
- benevolent; and
- related to behavior, not to personality.

Dealing with student feedback

"I analyze 25 questionnaires, and then I have no idea what to do with the results." This feedback from a seminar participant expresses a common problem: While there is now a wide range of qualitatively very different instruments available for feedback surveys, there is still hardly any information on the next step: Using feedback to implement change. In addition to the use of suitable survey tools, these questions are key factors in determining whether student feedback leads to positive effects for all involved: How can I use the information gained for further work? What can I do with the information I have received from my students?

Initially, when you get the feedback consider whether there is a need for change in your lessons and what conditions are helpful (and not helpful) for successful change.

The collection of student feedback is the first step in a process of self-reflection, but the use of feedback does not end there. Rather, the decisive phase occurs *after* the collection: dealing with the results and the subsequent consequences. Student feedback leads to professional development if it is accompanied by an adequate process of peer exchange and counseling (Roche & Marsh, 2002). Effective observable and even measurable changes in a student's perception of teaching results from specific interventions with the aim of improving teaching (Hativa, 1996).

The better the feedback is, the more interesting and lasting the exchange between students and the teacher can be. Thus, the discussion of the information gained provides further insights that teachers can use when planning their instruction. The next round of feedback can then focus on the changes implemented and determining whether they were effective in improving the quality of instruction. This is the secret of the success of feedback: It is the ticket to dialogue. It is an expression of mutual respect and appreciation. It helps to make learning visible and to optimize teaching for the benefit of students.

Collecting feedback is followed by generating useful results. It should be noted that the time required for analyzing data increases with increasing differentiation of questionnaires. From a practical point of view, it is unlikely that paper–pencil surveys, which require teachers to use a spreadsheet to generate meaningful results, are useful as instruments for regular student feedback (although they may be used selectively). Digital solutions minimize the effort required to collect and analyze data to a minimum, while at the same time reveal findings that are difficult or impossible to make visible without them. For example, it is quick and easy to use an app (such as that available on www.visiblefeedback.com) to offer a comprehensive questionnaire to students and to get meaningful results in a matter of seconds.

Feedback is never obtained for its own sake

Using feedback to make a behavioral change is the most important step in the entire feedback process. Feedback is never obtained for its own sake but always serves as a data-supported tool for reflecting on and adapting one's own behavior.

A common but rather unhelpful phenomenon is that many teachers ask for student feedback only at the end of the school year, sometimes in the last lesson before the summer holidays. Accordingly, feedback is understood as a kind of final evaluation. But who benefits from this? If feedback is supposed to support dialogue on teaching and learning, then this kind of final evaluation is inappropriate, because the results cannot be discussed with the class. The students provide feedback, but it is clear to them that their feedback will no longer affect them. For this reason, student feedback should not primarily be understood as a summative final evaluation (which has a low effect size) but rather as a formative process (with a high effect size, cf. Hattie & Zierer, 2017) that serves as an opportunity for discussion and change. This leads to an important principle of using feedback successfully: All feedback is the subject of a subsequent discussion between feedback providers and feedback recipients, and the objective of the feedback is transparent for all participants.

Dangers of feedback

Although student feedback, like any form of feedback, can lead to teachers' more accurate self-awareness, it carries the risk of adverse effects and even a decrease in performance by the feedback recipient (Kluger & DeNisi, 1996). Feedback can be misunderstood and used incorrectly, leading to a rejection of the information gained or to the shielding of one's own point of view (Atwater & Brett, 2005). In addition, the discrepancy between the feedback recipient's own goals and the feedback one has received can lead to a reduction in the experience of self-efficacy, standards, and self-satisfaction (Bandura & Locke 2003; Atwater & Brett, 2005). In short, whether feedback leads to pleased teachers and contented students in the end, or whether it is ineffective – if not counterproductive – depends not least on how the results are dealt with.

The process of responding to feedback begins with a constructive dialogue between the feedback provider and the feedback recipient, continues with targeted changes, and is usually followed by an evaluation to determine its success – which in turn leads to a dialogue on teaching and learning. It is a cyclical process (Figure 4.15).

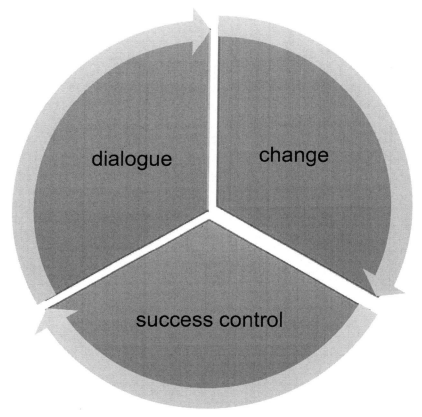

FIGURE 4.15 The process following feedback

It is a misunderstanding – unfortunately not an uncommon one – to understand feedback as an assessment or even a grading of one's own performance as a teacher (cf. Chapter 3). If this happens, the feedback does not offer an opportunity for change. It is helpful to use student feedback as information about one's own impact as a teacher. Criteria-driven, systematic feedback usually identifies many areas that learners perceive as positive.

Feedback points to resources

Student feedback often provides encouraging signals that motivate teachers to do their job. This is sometimes overlooked when feedback is put on a level with criticism. Nevertheless, any feedback can also contain aspects that are critical and suggest a change. Unfortunately, identifying opportunities for improvement, formulating appropriate target criteria, and drafting measures to achieve them are repeatedly met with fear and resistance in the school system (Warwas et al., 2008).

Feedback-based changes can affect small details, but they can also go deep. Changes can be carried out in a short time or take up a longer period of time. But no matter what a teacher wants to change, adjustments always involve self-reflection and potentially affect self-esteem. For this reason, change can be associated with emotions – both negative (fear, worry, anger, frustration, disappointment) and positive (joy, interest, satisfaction, euphoria). To avoid negative emotions and promote positive ones, one can either make a productive change or re-interpret the feedback. Such reinterpretation can be based on various cognitive processes.

Cognitive dissonance

"What nonsense! You think you can judge for yourself." Feedback may conflict with your own perception. Cognitive dissonance (Festinger et al., 1978) occurs when two cognitions that appear incompatible with each other occur simultaneously. This dissonance is perceived as unpleasant; it exerts pressure, and must therefore be reduced. One can do this by changing the cognition that requires the least amount of change but also by suppressing, ignoring, or adding new consonant information.

Reactance

"Don't tell me what to do!" Reactance refers to the attitude that forms the basis of a complex defensive reaction that occurs in response to external or internal constraints (Brehm, 1966). It can be shown that reactance occurs especially in people who are in urgent need of a change. These individuals in particular increasingly adhere to behavioral patterns (Behnke, 2015). In other words: The more other people would like someone to change, the less he or she is willing to do so.

Functional attachment

"I've always done it like that!" Functional fixedness prevents people from solving problems adequately, since behavior takes place in predefined ways, preventing adaptations to a changed situation from taking place. The change meets with rejection or is devalued or not considered irrelevant, because it disturbs the status quo and often forces people out of their comfort zones (Landes & Steiner, 2014).

Self-serving bias

"Students should look at their own problems instead of mine." Self-serving bias is a classic and frequently occurring distortion of perception. Failure is attributed to external factors that cannot be controlled by the person. Reactions to feedback tend to be carried out in such a way that one's self-esteem is protected or increased (Dauenheimer et al., 1997).

Whether a realistic self-perception or an increase in self-esteem takes place largely depends on the changeability of the behavior in question. People who believe that they can change their behavior are less affected by negative feedback and have an increased interest in receiving feedback on this aspect (Sedikides & Gregg, 2009, cited from Behnke, 2015). Creating motivation for change involves meeting two prerequisites (Schmitz, 2000): the conviction that the situation can be improved by the change (action–result expectation) and the conviction that one's own competence makes it possible to implement the change (self-efficacy expectation). In other words: First, there must be an mindframe that a change will improve things, and second, there must be a high level of perceived competence in making the change. This is shown in Figure 4.16.

Student feedback in practice

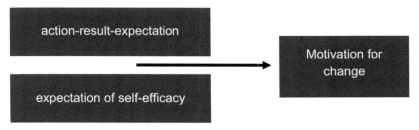

FIGURE 4.16 Conditions for change
Source: Schmitz (2000).

If there is a motivation to change, the next step is to plan the exact steps. This planning can be carried out by the teacher alone, in tandem, or in a group, depending on the complexity. Organizational psychology may be helpful at this point, as it looks at the topic of change in businesses. A number of findings can be transferred to the school system.

SWOT analysis

Changes can be planned in a structured form by conducting a (S)trengths (W)eakness (O)pportunities (T)hreats analysis (Stolzenberg & Heberle, 2006). The goal of the change process must be clear (e.g., "I want to involve my students more in the lessons," "I want to reduce the number of disturbances in my lessons," "I want to convey more content per lesson," etc.). An analysis is then performed with the help of the four fields shown in Table 4.4.

After answering these questions, one can develop a strategy and make a distinction between four basic types of strategies:

- "Expanding": utilization of existing resources in connection with existing opportunities.
- "Catching up": deriving opportunities from existing difficulties.
- "Hedging": using strengths to counteract risks.
- "Avoidance": preventing difficulties and risks from occurring at the same time.

The student feedback shown in Figure 4.14 would, for example, suggest the strategies "expanding" and "catching up." The fact that the students perceive teaching as extremely varied and interesting (resource) but at the same time the teacher still uses too little information on the actual

TABLE 4.4 Structured planning of a change process based on the SWOT analysis

PRESENT	
Strengths	**Weaknesses**
➤ What positive feedback did I get?	➤ Which problem(s) has/have been identified by the students?
➤ What feedback have I enjoyed?	
➤ What feedback made me proud?	➤ What do the students miss?
➤ What feedback motivates me?	➤ What is difficult for me?
	➤ What feedback hurts me?

FUTURE	
Opportunities	**Threats**
➤ What am I not using enough?	➤ Where are the risks of change?
➤ What can I enhance?	➤ What undesirable developments do I fear?
➤ Where do I have unused potential?	
➤ What support can I use?	

Source: Stolzenberg and Heberle (2006).

learning requirements of the students (chance) suggests the strategy of using the ability to empathize with the students as a form of diagnostics and categorizing the learning goals for each lesson according to the students' levels of competence. At the same time, the non–optimal fit can become an opportunity to reduce the inappropriate learning pace (difficulty) by allowing the students to determine the pace on their own (chance).

A phased model of change

In the following, we use various feedback scenarios to explain how changes in one's own behavior as a teacher can take place. To this end, we present a model of change processes that comprises four levels(Wisniewski & Zierer, 2017b):

Level 1: Self-directed change of behavior

Level 2: Assisted change of behavior

Level 3: Utilization of coaching or counseling

Level 4: Changes at system level

This model is combined with a pedagogical expertise model developed in the context of Visible Learning (Figure 4.17; Hattie & Zierer, 2017, cf. Chapter 6).

Student feedback in practice

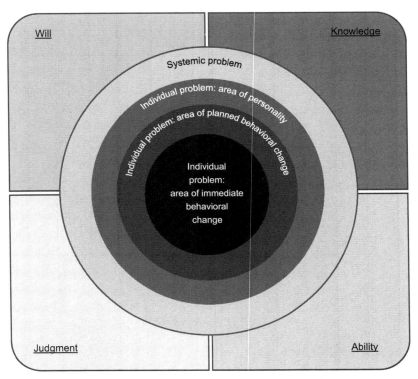

FIGURE 4.17 Levels of problems identified by student feedback

Level 1: self-directed change of behavior

This level of change occurs frequently in practice. At first glance, it represents a low threshold; for example, one might conclude from the feedback one gets from students that it is necessary or useful to adapt one's own behavior as a teacher. This change can be implemented directly and solely with one's own personal resources. It requires knowledge and abilities that the teacher already possesses or is able to acquire quickly, meaning that the levels that need to be reflected on are primarily those of will and judgment: Does the feedback make sense? Will I get involved in the feedback? At second glance, even this low-threshold form of change does not happen on its own but requires taking a significant step.

Example 1: A large part of a class reports back to the teacher that the homework review at the beginning of each lesson is inaccurate and that they are often unable to follow. On the basis of this feedback,

the teacher changes his lesson planning and spends more time on the homework review phase.

Example 2: A teacher frequently uses a certain word or phrase that causes students to laugh every time. This in turn leads to uncertainty in the teacher, as she does not know the cause of the laughter. Through student feedback, she is made aware of the frequent use and can reduce or eliminate the habit.

Level 2: assisted change of behavior

The next level also aims at adapting one's own behavior, but in contrast to Level 1, it acknowledges that a goal-oriented change is not possible without the addition of external resources such as, for example, cooperation with a colleague. At Level 2, an in-depth analysis of subject-based, didactic, and pedagogical aspects is often necessary. In this respect, the focus is on competence in the form of knowledge and ability. For example, a teacher discusses the feedback results with a colleague to get ideas on how he or she can improve a certain problematic situation. Time-intensive cooperation activities, in which a problem is solved or new strategies are worked out together, are relatively rare in everyday school life (Richter & Pant, 2016). Few teachers state that their school has a development or training plan for teachers to improve their professionalism. This is an indicator that there is a lack of support systems for teachers who want to develop. Nonetheless, collegial support systems are the most likely means of creating opportunities for exchange, experimentation, and learning from each other (Holtappels, 2013).

Example 3: A large part of a class reports back that lessons are often unstructured and incoherent. In a debriefing, first with the class and then with a confidant, the teacher works out strategies to increase the degree of structuring and coherence of the lessons, including writing the specific learning objectives on the blackboard at the beginning of each lesson, intermediate repetitions after each lesson phase, and providing a summary at the end of each lesson.

Example 4: A teacher receives feedback that he focuses too much on individual students and does not include the rest of the class. Here too, another teacher can be called upon to help develop possible solutions. In the debriefing, it is clarified that the focus on a few students is based on the fact that they are very active and often provide very fast and good contributions, especially for more complex tasks, while a large part of the class is rather passive and the teacher has to wait a long time for answers. A strategy is developed in which short individual or

partner work phases are regularly incorporated into the teaching process before more complex tasks or questions are given to the students, so that they have time to prepare an appropriate response.

Level 3: utilization of coaching or counseling

At Level 3, student feedback (sometimes repeatedly) refers to a teacher's specific dysfunctional behavior, which may lead to more severe impairments of the teaching process. A largely self-directed change of behavior as on the first two levels is not possible, since the causes of the problem are unknown to the feedback recipient and/or also lie in stable personality aspects. For this reason, it makes sense at this stage to use professional support systems, which offer the opportunity of illuminating problems from different perspectives within a confidential and protected framework and ensuring that teachers are accompanied by a specially trained person. Consequently, the process of change refers to all areas of professionalization and requires an intensive exchange and dialogue, both in terms of competencies and mindframes. All this can be done within the framework of coaching or counseling. It has long been known that these support systems are highly effective for complex change processes (Guskey, 1986). The infrequent use of professional support systems within the school system is due to the fact that many teachers still see asking for help as a taboo (cf., e.g., Scala & Grossmann, 1997; Petrovic, 2010). It is precisely for this reason that confidentiality is of the utmost importance here.

Example 5: A teacher gets the feedback that the students do not understand the content of her lessons, because they cannot follow her way of explaining things. The learners perceive the lessons to be "over their heads" and have severe problems following them. In this case, there is a complex problem about the teaching behavior that is closely related to the competence of the teacher and requires far-reaching changes. As a result, it would be important for the teacher to question her own view of what constitutes an age-appropriate and conclusive way of explaining things within the framework of group coaching and to receive suggestions for alternative approaches from colleagues and a specialist.

Example 6: A teacher faces severe disciplinary difficulties in several classes. The students report that there are no recognizable rules and procedures and that the teacher is often vague in his communication. Various self-chosen measures for improvement did not lead to positive consequences. It becomes clear that the problems that arise are primarily the result of inconsistent instructional behavior, the causes of which lie partly in personality traits of the teacher (who is has a high level of introversion). Within the framework of a one-on-one coaching session, the teacher can reflect on existing behavioral patterns and then learn and practice new, more functional ways of behavior that make it easier for him to manage the classroom.

Level 4: changes at system level

Level 4 refers to changes that not only affect the individual teacher but are also more far-reaching. Student feedback can show that it is not the behavior of a single person but problematic systemic conditions that cause certain difficulties. In this case, it is not enough for an individual teacher to change his or her behavior, but it is necessary to take measures across the entire institution in order to bring about a successful change. This requires systemic professionalism. Teachers must know where to apply the change in the system and must be motivated to do so. In this respect, competence and mindframes are required. For effective changes to take place at the system level, certain conditions must be met. An overview of the conditions of successful and less successful changes can be found in Table 4.5.

Example 7: Students report back over time that they cannot concentrate because they are distracted by disturbances caused by some classmates. However, the problem in this case does not affect a single teacher but occurs in many different contexts. The disturbances are caused by several students who have been diagnosed with attention deficit disorders. This problem therefore requires measures that go

TABLE 4.5 Success-critical factors of change processes at the systemic level

SUCCESSFUL CHANGE	LESS SUCCESSFUL CHANGE
task force that accompanies the process with commitment systematic exchange of experience open communication between the participants	lack of support systems/delayed adoption of management systems chaotic process/insufficient planning lack of systemic thinking, lack of transparency

Source: Warwas et al. (2008).

beyond an individual teacher's behavioral change. For example, the entire staff could be trained to deal with attention disorders.

Example 8: In this final example, critical student feedback refers to the area of consolidation. Learners report that they have few opportunities to practice new content, especially in the core subjects. As in Example 7, this feedback affects several teachers. The problem perceived and described by the students has systemic causes: It is difficult for several colleagues to structure their lessons in such a way that there is enough time for practice. If this is a structural problem, we need to consider how the systemic conditions can be changed. At the system level, for example, it would be conceivable to change the lesson schedule from 45-minute units to 90-minute units, so that practice phases can be integrated more easily into the lessons.

Measurement of success

Success is difficult to define in the teaching profession and can only be measured in the long term. While a doctor almost immediately sees whether an operation has been successful, an engineer can easily evaluate whether a construction is working, and a lawyer learns quickly whether he or she has won a lawsuit, some teachers will have to wait until the graduation ceremony to hear: "We've really learned a lot from you." Teachers usually don't see immediate results of their daily work and therefore are not always aware of the fact that when making changes, the immediate results of these changes need to be checked. Consequently, it is especially important to keep an eye on success control and to make the learning process and teaching success visible again and again.

In the context of student feedback, the most concrete measurement of success is obtained by another request for student feedback after the change has been implemented. If the student feedback reveals a positive change attributable to the teacher's actions, this leads to a feeling of self-efficacy. At the same time, the motivation to keep up a dialogue with students about teaching and learning increases. It is necessary to formulate clearly defined goals that teachers want to accomplish in a way that they are challenging, transparent, and verifiable (cf. Hattie and Zierer, 2017). According to Rogers (1995), good goals require transparency concerning the standard, the condition under which performance is to be achieved, and the observable behavior. With these considerations, goals become criteria for success – and thus the yardstick for one's own professionalism.

Student feedback in practice

Feedback is particularly effective when given by students to teachers. Feedback can be obtained in different ways. Criteria-guided, evidence-based, and validated questionnaire instruments are particularly helpful. Since these are associated with processing effort, digital solutions are the ideal solution for a practical implementation.

Student feedback always serves as an introduction to a dialogue between students and teachers. Therefore, it is essential to discuss the feedback results with the students and to clarify the actual changes that result from the feedback.

For feedback providers, it is important to ensure that feedback recipients can accept feedback and use it for change. For this purpose, feedback should primarily relate to behavior and be substantiated.

The question of how to deal with feedback cannot be answered in a prescription (such as "If you get this feedback, then do this"). As almost always in the educational context, the success of measures depends on many different factors. Sometimes – probably much more often than teachers would suspect – the answer to the question can simply be "Go on!" or "More of it!" because with all the criticism that feedback can bring, it is also often a confirmation of the daily work done by teachers and a relativization of selective criticism.

Bibliography

Atwater, L. E., & Brett, J. F. (2005). Antecedents and consequences of reactions to developmental 360 feedback. *Journal of Vocational Behavior*, 66(3), 532–548.

Balch, R. T. (2012). *The validation of a student survey on teacher practice*. Nashville, TN: Vanderbilt University Press.

Bandura, A., & Locke, E. A. (2003). Negative self-efficacy and goal effects revisited. *Journal of Applied Psychology*, 88(1), 87.

Behnke, K. (2015). Umgang mit Feedback im Kontext Schule. *Erkenntnisse aus Analysen der externen Evaluation und des Referendariats*. Wiesbaden: Springer.

Bennett, B., & Smilanich, P. (1994). *Classroom management: Thinking & caring approach*. Toronto: Bookation.

Braun, E., & Leidner, B. (2009). Academic course evaluation: Theoretical and empirical distinctions between self-rated gain in competences and satisfaction with teaching behavior. *European Psychologist*, 14(4), 297–306.

Brehm, J. W. (1966). *Theory of psychological reactance*. New York: Academic Press.

Dauenheimer, D., Stahlberg, D., & Petersen, L. E. (1997). Reaktionen auf Leistungsbewertungen in Abhängigkeit vom Elaborationsgrad des

Selbstbildes und der Motivation zur Veränderung. *Zeitschrift für Sozialpsychologie, 28,* 19–29.

Festinger, L., Irle, M., & Möntmann, V. (1978). *Theorie der kognitiven Dissonanz.* Bern: Huber.

Frommer, H., & Bovet, G. (1999). *Praxis Lehrerberatung-Lehrerbeurteilung: Konzepte für Ausbildung und Schulaufsicht.* Baltmannsweiler: Schneider.

Gates Foundation. (2012). *Asking students about teaching: Student perception surveys and their implementation.* MET Project Policy and Practice Summary. Colorado: Bill & Melinda Gates Foundation.

Gates Foundation. (2013). *Ensuring fair and reliable measures of effective teaching. Culminating findings from MET project's three year study.* Online www.metpro ject.org/downloads/MET_Ensuring _Fair_and_Reliable_Measures_ Practitioner_Brief.pdf, [14.12.2014].

Gruehn, S. (2000). Unterricht und schulisches Lernen. *Schüler als Quellen der Unterrichtsbeschreibung.* Waxmann: Verlag.

Guskey, T. R. (1986). Staff development and the process of teacher change. *Educational Researcher, 15*(5), 5–12.

Hativa, N. (1996). University instructors' ratings profiles: Stability over time, and disciplinary differences. *Research in Higher Education, 37*(3), 241–265.

Hattie, J. (2008). *Visible Learning: A synthesis of over 800 meta-analyses relating to achievement.* London: Routledge.

Hattie, J. (2013). *Visible learning for teachers.* London: Routledge.

Hattie, J., & Zierer, K. (2017). *10 mindframes for visible learning: Teaching for success.* London: Routledge.

Holtappels, H. G. (2013). Schulentwicklung und Lehrerkooperation. *Empirische Bildungsforschung. Theorien, Methoden, Befunde und Perspektiven,* 35–62.

Hynds, A. (2010). Unpacking resistance to change within-school reform programmes with a social justice orientation. *International Journal of Leadership in Education, 13,* 377–392.

Kanning, U. P., & Rustige, J. (2012). Der Stellenwert von Feedback-Regeln aus empirischer Sicht. *Personalführung, 5,* 24–31.

Kluger, A. N., & DeNisi, A. (1996). The effects of feedback interventions on performance: A historical review, a meta-analysis, and a preliminary feedback intervention theory. *Psychological Bulletin, 119*(2), 254.

Landes, M., & Steiner, E. (2014). *Psychologische Auswirkungen von Change Prozessen: Widerstände, Emotionen, Veränderungsbereitschaft und Implikationen für Führungskräfte.* Heidelberg: Springer-Verlag.

Latane, B. (1981). The psychology of social impact. *American psychologist, 36*(4), 343.

Lenske, G. (2016). *Schülerfeedback in der Grundschule: Untersuchung zur Validität.* Münster: Waxmann.

Lorenz, M. (2014). *Praktische Psychologie für den Umgang mit Mitarbeitern: Wirkungsvoll und leistungsorientiert führen.* Hamburg: Springer.

Moosbrugger, H., & Kelava, A. (2007). *Testtheorie und Fragebogenkonstruktion.* Heidelberg: Springer.

Onwuegbuzie, A. J., Daniel, L. G., & Collins, K. M. (2009). A meta-validation model for assessing the score-validity of student teaching evaluations. *Quality & Quantity*, 43(2), 197–209.

Petrovic, S. (2010). *Supervision an Schulen* (Dissertation, University of Vienna, Vienna).

Richter, D., & Pant, H. A. (2016). *Lehrerkooperation in Deutschland. Eine Studie zu kooperativen Arbeitsbeziehungen bei Lehrkräften der Sekundarstufe I*. Gütersloh: Robert Bosch Stiftung.

Roche, L. A., & Marsh, H. W. (2002). Teaching self-concept in higher education. In N. Hativa & J. Goodyear(Eds.), *Teacher thinking, beliefs and knowledge in higher education*. Dordrecht, Netherlands: Springer. 179–218.

Rogers, E. (1995). *The diffusion of innovations*. New York: Free Press.

Scala, K., & Grossmann, R. (1997). *Supervision in Organisationen. Veränderungen bewältigen – Qualität sichern – Entwicklung fördern*. München: Juventa.

Schmitz, G. S. (2000). *Zur Struktur und Dynamik der Selbstwirksamkeitserwartung von Lehrern: Ein protektiver Faktor gegen Belastung und Burnout?* (Dissertation paper, Free University of Berlin, Berlin).

Schnell, R., Hill, P., & Esser, E. (2005). *Methoden der empirischen Sozialforschung*. München: Oldenbourg.

Schönbächler, M. T. (2008). Klassenmanagement: situative Gegebenheiten und personale Faktoren in Lehrpersonen-und Schülerperspektive (Vol. 7). Bern: Haupt Verlag AG.

Sedikides, C., & Gregg, A. P. (2009). Self-enhancement: Food for thought. *Perspectives on Psychological Science*, 3(2), 102–116.

Stolzenberg, K., & Heberle, K. (2006). *Change Management: Veränderungsprozesse erfolgreich gestalten, Mitarbeiter mobilisieren*. Heidelberg: Springer.

Strahm, P. (2008). *Qualität durch systematisches Feedback: Grundlagen, Einblicke und Werkzeuge*. Bern: Schulverlag blmv.

Warwas, J., Seifried, J., & Meier, M. (2008). *Change Management von Schulen: Erfolgsfaktoren und Handlungsstrategien aus Sicht der Schulleitung an beruflichen Schulen*. Gernsbach: Deutscher Betriebswirte-Verlag.

Wisniewski, B. (2016). Vom fundierten Wissen zur reflektierten Praxis – Möglichkeiten und Grenzen der Professionalisierung in der Lehrerbildung. *Schulmagazin 5–10*, 11/2016, 11–14.

Wisniewski, B., & Zierer, K. (2016). Schulentwicklung nach Hattie. *SchulVerwaltung BY*, 12/2016, 343–346.

Wisniewski, B., & Zierer, K. (2017a). Schülerfeedback ist nicht gleich Schülerfeedback. *PÄDAGOGIK*, 11(17), 38–42.

Wisniewski, B., & Zierer, K. (2017b). Schülerfeedback: und dann? *SchulVerwaltung BY*, 12/2017, 24–33.

Wisniewski, B., & Zierer, K. (in preparation). *Entwicklung und Validierung eines Online-Fragebogens (teaCh) für Schülerfeedback*.

CHAPTER 5

Student feedback scenarios using digitization

To provide suggestions for using student feedback and to put into practice the previous remarks on implementation, the following four scenarios illustrate what the feedback process can look like in reality. In all examples, feedback was obtained with the software available on www.visiblefeedback.com. This shows how digitization facilitates effective use of feedback in schools.

Readers can visit the website www.visiblefeedback.com to use a free trial version of the online teaCh questionnaire. The website offers the opportunity to give feedback on statements on the basis of a four-level scale of 1: "I don't agree," 2: "I rather don't agree," 3: "I rather agree," and 4: "I agree" (Figure 5.1).

The items are grouped into superordinate categories. For example, the category "Clarify" contains the following items.

Clarify

The teacher exactly told me what I was supposed to learn during this lesson
The teacher expressed herself/himself precisely.
The lesson was coherent.
The items are formulated in such a way that "I agree" is always the desirable option. This is additionally illustrated by smileys.

Free-text entries are also possible, either for answers on specific items or in general. The results of questionnaire surveys are displayed graphically in three variants.

| I don't agree | I rather don't agree | I rather agree | I agree |

FIGURE 5.1 Four-step response option for questionnaire items

First, barometers are displayed for all requested categories. These offer the most general form of presentation and give an initial overview of which areas have been perceived as positive or more negative. The barometer shows the average of all responses within a category (Figure 5.2).

Second, perspectives are compared. Here, the students' response and the teacher's self-perception are compared within each category. Figure 5.3 compares the perception of a teacher (upper, heavy line) and the average perception of a group of students (lower, lighter line). The dots represent the average item answer on a scale of 1 to 4 ("I don't agree" to "I agree"). On the leftmost side of the x-axis, for example, you can see that the teacher perceived Item 7 to be 4: "I agree," and the students perceived it to be 1.9 (the average of all student responses is displayed here), which is just below "I rather don't agree."

Third, a response distribution shows how often which response alternative was chosen for each item (Figure 5.4). This helps the teacher to determine how homogenously or heterogeneously the item was answered. The mean value in the comparison of perspectives does not provide any information on how the perception of the feedback providers is distributed. For example, an average of 2.5 can be the consequence of half of the respondents selecting "I rather don't agree" and half selecting "I rather agree" but also of half of the respondents selecting "I don't agree" and half selecting "I agree." The interpretation of these two variants would have to be completely different.

Student feedback: classroom climate

In the first example, at a secondary school, 19 eighth-grade students completed a questionnaire on classroom climate.

Questionnaire: classroom climate
Goal: gaining information for a class council about collaboration
Level: process

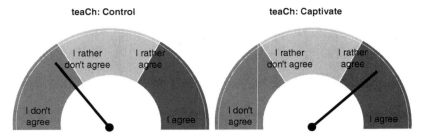

FIGURE 5.2 Feedback barometers

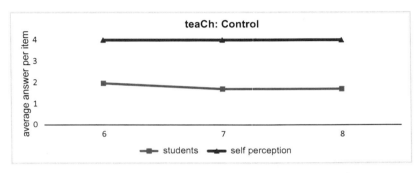

1: I don't agree • 2: I rather don't agree • 3: I rather agree • 4: I agree • 0: no answer

FIGURE 5.3 Comparison of perspectives

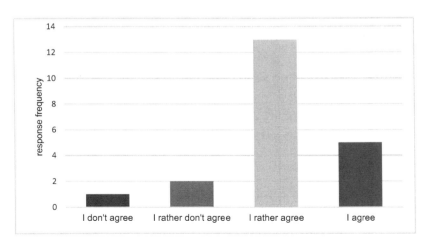

FIGURE 5.4 Response distribution

The motivation for the class teacher was that previous class council sessions did not lead to a real discussion with the students on several occasions, as there was no concrete reason for the discussion and they then expressed general criticism of various circumstances in a very unstructured manner. The conversation was also strongly dominated by individual opinions.

The class teacher made the questionnaire available online one week before a class council was held in order to get an impression of the atmosphere and to find out which topics were relevant for the class.

Questionnaire 1: Classroom climate

Teacher–student relationships

1. There is a pleasant atmosphere in my class.
2. The teachers are personally interested in me.
3. My teachers treat me fairly.
4. My classmates and I have opportunities for participation.
5. My teachers like me.
6. I can learn without pressure.
7. I get feedback from my teachers about where I have improved and where I need to work harder.
8. My teachers are working hard to make me improve.

Student–student relationships

9. In my class, we learn and work without competition or rivalry.
10. My classmates and I help each other.
11. I'm well integrated in my class.
12. My classmates and I are a community without cliques.
13. We students treat each other with respect.

The results were presented and discussed in the class council session (Figure 5.5). The class teacher first pointed out the positive perceptions of the students and then addressed the two negatively perceived areas. These were Iem 6, "I can learn without pressure," in the category

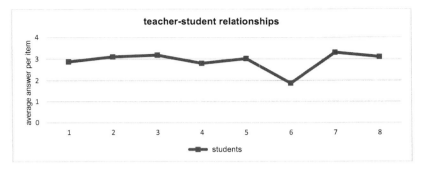

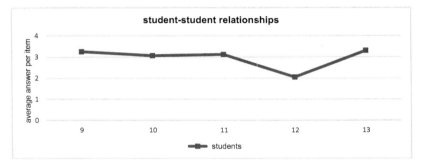

FIGURE 5.5 Results of the questionnaire on the classroom climate

"teacher–student relationships" and Item 15, "My classmates and I are a community without cliques," in the category "student–student relationships." Both are marked as numbers on the x-axis.

It turned out that 16 out of 19 students fully or somewhat disagreed with the statement "I can learn without pressure"; 13 out of 19 students also disagreed with the statement "My classmates and I are a community without cliques." Here, the proportion of "I don't agree" responses was even higher.

The responses to these two items were further substantiated by the students in the class council session. They described that tests were often scheduled extremely tightly. They also told the class teacher that there were three classmates who had little contact with the others and were sometimes even treated in a hostile way (Figure 5.6).

The class teacher had the students collect ideas for the two points in small groups, which were then presented to the plenary of the class council. This resulted in numerous ideas, from which the following were selected by vote.

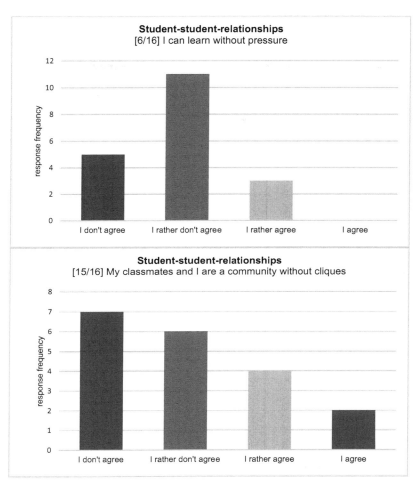

FIGURE 5.6 Response distribution

	TEACHERS	STUDENTS
Problem 1	• Better coordination in setting examination dates	
Problem 2	• Implementation of a team-building measure in the form of team training	• Creation of a class album for getting to know each other better • Formation of a group at an online chat room for the whole class • Election of a student to be in charge of integration

After six weeks, the classroom climate questionnaire was released to allow the success of the measures to be reviewed.

Student feedback: general instructional quality

The second example shows student feedback on teaching in the sixth grade of a secondary school. It refers to a grammar lesson in English, in which conditional sentences were introduced.

> Questionnaire: instructional quality
> Objective: reflection on the teacher's behavior
> Level: process and self-regulation

The feedback was carried out without any special goal, and the aim was to get a general impression of how teaching is perceived by the class.

The English teacher asked her students to fill out a teaCh questionnaire on instructional quality and gave a self-estimation. The questionnaire contains a total of 29 items on the categories of "Care," "Challenge," "Clarify," "Control," "Captivate," "Confer," and "Consolidate." Following is one of the categories.

Questionnaire 2: Quality of teaching (extract from teaCh)

Clarify

1. The teacher has repeated content from the previous lessons.
2. The teacher has tied in content that was already known to me.
3. Before introducing new content, the teacher checked whether I had the necessary prior knowledge.
4. The teacher showed me what the new content is related to.
5. The teacher has shown me what I can use the new content for.
6. The teacher told me exactly what I should learn in this lesson.
7. The teacher has expressed himself in a precise and understandable way.
8. The lesson had a clearly recognizable thread.

Student feedback scenarios using digitization

An initial overview of the results shows that the students mostly agreed with the items in "Challenge" and "Care," tended to agree with the items in "Clarify," and did not agree or disagreed with the items in "Consolidate." The barometers (Figure 5.7) show the category mean value.

A comparison of the perspectives shows clearly that there are significant deviations between the teacher's self-estimation and the perception of the class for two items in "Clarify" (on the x-axis), namely Item 1 ("The teacher has repeated content from the previous lessons") and Item 6 ("The teacher has told me exactly what I was supposed to learn in this lesson") (Figure 5.8). However, the assessment of students in the whole category "Challenge" was much more favorable than the teacher's self-estimation.

The results were discussed with the class in the next lesson. The teacher showed the class the deviations and asked for possible reasons (Figure 5.9). The class gave the following reasons:

- At the beginning of the lesson, the teacher reviewed the content of the preliminary lesson by questioning one student. Many of the other students were mentally absent at that time and were therefore not aware of the review.
- The teacher had introduced the topic "conditional sentences" with a cartoon that was talked about for a long time and which was not

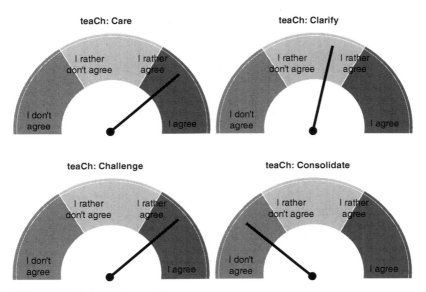

FIGURE 5.7 Category barometers

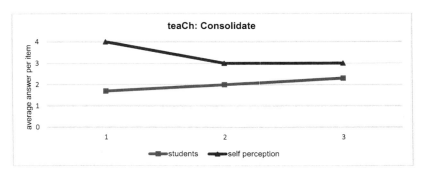

1: I don't agree • 2: I rather don't agree • 3: I rather agree • 4: I agree • 0: no answer

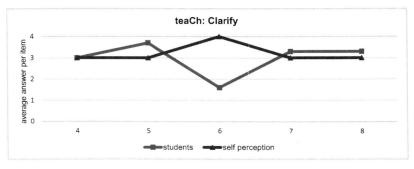

1: I don't agree • 2: I rather don't agree • 3: I rather agree • 4: I agree • 0: no answer

FIGURE 5.8 Comparison of perspectives

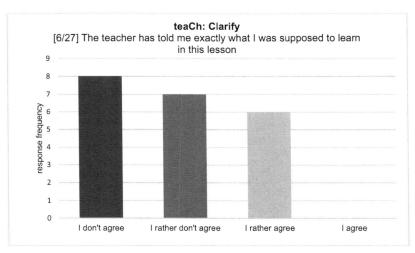

FIGURE 5.9 Response distribution

Student feedback scenarios using digitization

comprehensible to all students. As a result, they didn't know what the lesson was all about.
- The cartoon distracted the students from the actual topic rather than creating motivation.
- The topic of the lesson was only explicitly mentioned very late.

For further grammar lessons, the teacher made the following changes to the lesson plan:

- activation of all students in the review phase;
- clear indication of the lesson topic and lesson goals at the beginning of each lesson; and
- clear connection of all lesson elements to the actual learning objective.

Student feedback: specific aspects of a lesson

A teacher would like to find out why her ninth-grade German class is not motivated to learn the subject. In contrast to her other, younger classes, she is not able to inspire the students in this class, even though it is a strong class. In this example, she collected student feedback to find out why.

Questionnaire: specific aspects of teaching
Objective: to gain information about the lack of student participation
Level: process and self-regulation

Questionnaire 3: Items from the categories "Challenge" (extract from teaCh)

Challenge

1 The tasks were challenging for me.
2 The requirements of the lesson were appropriate for me.
3 The teacher had high expectations of me.

The comparison between the teacher's self-estimation and the students' feedback showed that there were large deviations for items 1, 3, and 4 (on the x-axis), that is, for the areas that affect the level of difficulty set by the teacher (Figure 5.10).

89

Student feedback scenarios using digitization

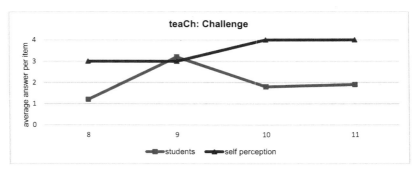

1: I don't agree • 2: I rather don't agree • 3: I rather agree • 4: I agree • 0: no answer

FIGURE 5.10 Comparison of perspectives

For this purpose, she selected 11 items from the "Challenge" and "Captivate" categories from the teaCh questionnaire and gave the students the opportunity to comment on each item freely.

The response distribution for the problematic items showed that the teacher's expectations and the level of difficulty were perceived as unfavorable by almost the entire class (Figure 5.11).

In addition to the student feedback on the predefined four-level scale from "I do not agree" to "I agree," the free-text comments shown in Table 5.1 were provided by the students.

This feedback indicates several existing motivational problems. A blind spot here was the perceived level of difficulty as too low, possibly due to the fact that the teacher worked predominantly in lower grades. Tasks are mainly assigned to the surface level (reproduction and reorganization) and only few to the transfer and problem solving level.

While the class evidently found the lessons to be interesting, varied, and practical, it was necessary to adjust the level of difficulty. For this reason, the teacher set her own goals for change:

- Reduce the reproductive portion of tasks in the classroom.
- Increase the transfer of tasks in the classroom.

The effectiveness of the changes was verified after six weeks with a repetition of the survey.

Student feedback: specific aspects of teaching

In this example, a teacher received feedback from an 11th grade class at a technical college. Prior to this, it was agreed that the feedback should

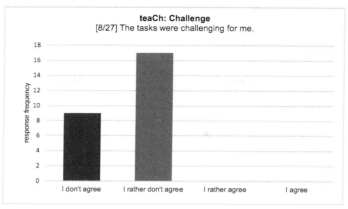

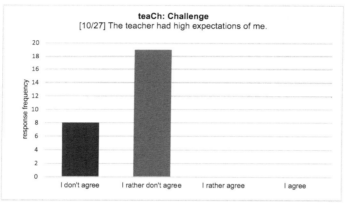

FIGURE 5.11 Response distribution

TABLE 5.1 Free-text annotations of students (selection)

Item 8	"You underestimate us!" "We're ninth graders, not fifth graders!" "You keep telling us we're not motivated, and that's not very motivating." "Please more discussion in class and less copying from the blackboard!" "Last school year we often had to justify our opinion, now we just have to learn by heart." "Often monotonous activities!"
Item 9	"Far too much repetition." "I'm NOT being challenged." "Too easy!"
Item 11	"When we present something, you never tell us if it was good or not." "I often don't even know if what I said was right or wrong."

focus on three core areas, namely "Control," "Care," and "Captivate." The feedback recipient wanted to find out why the students did not participate very much in her lessons.

Questionnaire: teaching quality
Objective: to gain information about the lack of class participation
Level: process and self-regulation

The students gave feedback on a mathematics lesson with the topic "calculation of probabilities." They answered a questionnaire on the three areas that had been previously agreed upon (14 items in total) via www.visiblefeedback.com. Using the same items, the teacher carried out a self-evaluation. The comparison of the two perspectives then served as a basis for the debriefing of the lesson, which took place the next day.

Questionnaire 4: Control and Confer (extract from teaCh)

Control

1 The teacher created an undisturbed learning atmosphere.
2 In the lesson, there were clear rules that the teacher set and enforced.
3 In the case of violations of the rules by students, the teacher intervened quickly and consistently.
4 The teacher had a good overview of what was going on in the classroom.
5 The teacher made me aware of what he or she expected me to do.

Confer

6 The teacher gave me the opportunity to get involved in the lessons.
7 The teacher was friendly and appreciative.
8 The teacher gave me meaningful feedback on my contributions.
9 The teacher gave me enough time to answer questions.

A comparison of the perspectives (Figure 5.12) shows that there was a high degree of agreement between the two estimations, although the teacher was more critical of the area of "Control," which the students perceived much more favorably. Within the category "Confer," however, it was noticeable that there were deviations in the assessment of Items 8 ("The teacher gave me meaningful feedback on my contributions") and 9 ("The teacher gave me enough time to answer questions").

These two items are relevant to the feedback recipient's initial question about the lack of participation in the class. The students' observation was that all too often there was only a very short period of time to think about the teachers' questions. That is why many students stopped engaging with the lesson. This effect was exacerbated by the teacher's poor differentiation and lack of meaningful feedback on students' contributions ("Mhm," "Good," "OK").

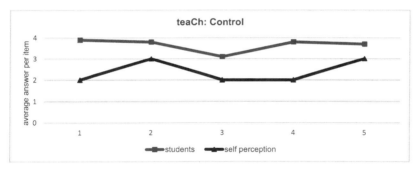

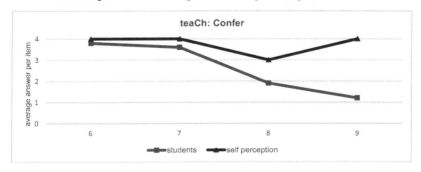

FIGURE 5.12 Comparison of perspectives

On the basis of these findings, the following points for altering the procedures were defined as agreed targets:

- use of individual and partner work phases in which answers can be prepared without time pressure;
- calling on as many different students as possible; and
- change of feedback to students to include at least one substantiated sentence instead of one-word phrases.

Thanks to digital instruments, the collection of meaningful and differentiated student feedback is also possible in a short amount of time. In this way, students' perceptions can be compared with self-perception in the shortest possible time, and suitable measures can be derived from it.

CHAPTER

6

Feedback culture and professionalism

Carefully consider these questions:

- What does "feedback culture" mean to you?
- How would you recognize a genuine feedback culture at your school?

This chapter deals with how feedback can become an integral part of individual teachers' approaches to teaching, but ideally change an entire school. Student feedback as it has been described in this book is effective only if appropriate mindframes are prevalent within a school.

What has become apparent in the previous chapters is to be considered separately again: Successful feedback is a question not only of competence but also of mindframes. It is therefore not enough to know how to and be able to give or receive feedback. Rather, the decisive factor is the motivation and the motives that make people do – or don't do – something. Thus, the final step is to explain the extent to which competence and mindframes are important for the development of a feedback culture.

After reading this chapter, you should

- be able to take a differentiated view of the term "feedback culture";
- know success factors for the implementation of feedback; and
- understand the relationship between feedback and professionalism.

Perhaps you have already asked yourself what head teachers or authorities actually mean when promoting the term "feedback culture." Do teachers give a lot of feedback or do they get a lot of feedback? If there is a feedback culture, do all members of the school

95

community know how to give feedback and how to deal with it? Are there regular training courses and pedagogical training days on this topic, and are both students and teachers familiar with feedback procedures? Are all those involved in school life asked for their opinion, including parents and non-pedagogical staff? Are there functioning channels of information and communication? As you can see, establishing a *real* feedback culture is not as simple as it might seem.

It is easy to see whether "feedback culture" is an empty phrase in schools or whether it is something that is in fact implemented. Schools that have established effective feedback mechanisms accomplish amazing changes. Talking about teaching and how teaching can make a change displaces the notion of being stuck in deficit orientation. An overall solution-oriented approach to everyday challenges leads not only to a higher student satisfaction but also to higher teacher satisfaction (Enns et al., 2004). Although in many cases student feedback is initially seen as a real threat because it does not seem to comply with the grammar of schooling, in reality it is often an important factor for job satisfaction. Unjustified complaints from parents can easily be refuted if they are not confirmed by student feedback – and justified complaints emerge to a lesser extent because they are prevented by the feedback process.

The way to a feedback culture

It goes without saying that a feedback culture is not established without difficulty. The implementation is a medium to long-term process. The introduction of student feedback as part of the school profile leads to prototypical phases such as those that occur when introducing innovations in general.

As can be seen in Figure 6.1, it is a long and stony road to the point where innovations such as student feedback become part of the collective self-concept of a system. As a rule, this usually leads through phases of shock and frustration to grief about the loss of the "good old days." If things go badly, the process ends there and the innovation fails. Typically, in this case the implementation isn't finished, followed by an admission of failure, but the project somehow comes to nothing. After a while you can say: "We tried, but it didn't work."

Alternatively, the low point will be followed by a period of openness associated with curiosity and enthusiasm, which will first manifest itself in a small group of innovators and early adopters and then spread so widely that a critical mass of early and late majority will be reached.

Feedback culture and professionalism

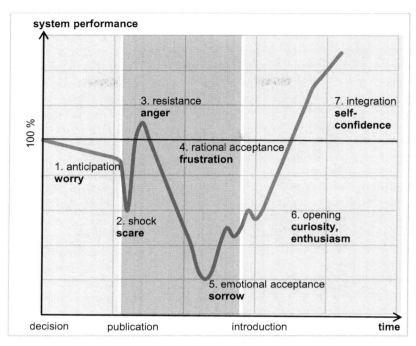

FIGURE 6.1 System performance when introducing innovations
Source: Roth (2000).

These processes can be described by diffusion theory (Rogers, 1995), which is illustrated in Figure 6.2. It is not a problem if a group of laggards remain who remain opposed to innovation for a long time or even permanently.

Every school board is faced with the question of how many members of the staff they have to win over in order to successfully launch a reform. In a similar way, teachers constantly consider how much approval is needed on the part of the students to initiate a successful learning process (see Hattie & Zierer, 2017). The frequent answer is 100%! Not only does this answer create tremendous pressure, but it is also wrong, as results from economics research show (cf. Endres & Martiensen 2007): It has been found that a company can achieve a monopoly position in the market starting not with 100%, not with 50%, but with between 20% to 30%. This shows that changes need only a relatively small critical mass in order to be successfully launched. In game theory, this is referred to as the "threshold value." Once this threshold has been achieved, change is set in motion without any further action, reforming an existing system and replacing it with a new

Feedback culture and professionalism

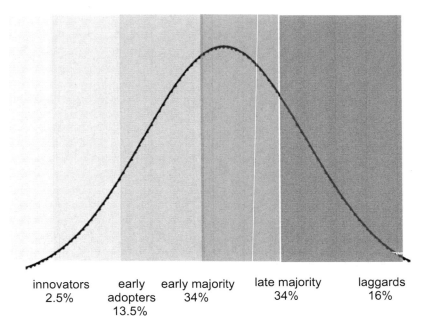

FIGURE 6.2 Innovation cycle
Source: Rogers (1995).

one. Research has shown that this effect can occur in group-dynamic processes and is therefore of interest for all forms of leadership. It will therefore be sufficient for a school board if they have won over a critical mass of people from their staff for their vision to be able to successfully put it into practice. It is not possible to determine the exact extent of this critical mass – although it is certain that it does not have to be 100%!

On the one hand this insight into the conditions for the success of changes has a relieving effect, and on the other hand it gives courage. It clarifies that it is worthwhile to initiate reforms, even if not everyone is convinced (yet). The critical mass is crucial for success!

According to Rogers (1995), whether innovations are ultimately accepted or rejected depends on the following five factors:

- Relative advantage: How does the individual perceive the improvement caused by innovation in comparison to the status quo?
- Compatibility: To what extent is the innovation compatible with previous experience, existing standards, and subjective needs?

- Complexity: How difficult is the implementation of innovation for individuals?
- Triability: To what extent is it possible to test the implementation, e.g., through the possibility of testing applications or through existing experience from other schools?
- Observability: Are the changes visible to the participants and the benefits perceptible?

The prerequisites for the establishment of an actual feedback culture are advantages that are clearly recognizable for teachers and students, a transparent coordination with all participants, the simplicity of implementation, and the opportunity to try out student feedback step-by-step.

An obstacle to innovations in the education sector is that teachers are frequently beset by "innovations" that are not based on evidence (cf. Chapter 2.1). Because there have been many innovations without any proven benefit – neither confirmed by research nor in practice by evaluation – some schools have become skeptical about innovation per se (cf., e.g., Terhart, 2002). Certainly, you can immediately think of some examples of innovations that have been forced upon you without benefit. The German proverb "a new pig is constantly being driven through the village" refers to the phenomenon of implementing many new innovations in short intervals. This hinders sensible innovations such as student feedback, the benefits of which have been clearly proven.

To sum it up, a feedback culture can be claimed when student feedback is accepted and implemented as part of the teaching reality by the overwhelming majority of the teaching staff of a school. To achieve this, certain success factors are important.

Success factors

The successful implementation of student feedback will depend on giving teachers good reasons why they should take this step. In Chapters 2 and 3 you have already learned some of these reasons, but maybe you will also find more for yourself.

In any case, it is advisable to address these reasons specifically – because we have reasons for everything, and this means that we also find reasons for what we don't want to do. So share your reasons and discuss your mindframes towards feedback at school. You can use the following questionnaire for this purpose (1 = do not agree at all up to 4 = agree fully).

> *Questionnaire 5: Feedback mindframes*
>
> | FEEDBACK MINDFRAMES | 1 | 2 | 3 | 4 |
> |---|---|---|---|---|
> | I give regular feedback. | ☐ | ☐ | ☐ | ☐ |
> | I am convinced that feedback is important. | ☐ | ☐ | ☐ | ☐ |
> | I look for feedback from colleagues on a regular basis. | ☐ | ☐ | ☐ | ☐ |
> | I look for regular feedback from the students. | ☐ | ☐ | ☐ | ☐ |
> | I can handle positive and negative feedback. | ☐ | ☐ | ☐ | ☐ |
> | A positive culture of error is important to me. | ☐ | ☐ | ☐ | ☐ |
> | Learning and teaching means making mistakes. | ☐ | ☐ | ☐ | ☐ |
> | Teaching means seeing learning through the eyes of the students. | ☐ | ☐ | ☐ | ☐ |

Comprehensive information for all parties involved is essential. Not only do the teachers need an introduction, but the students also need to be informed about why they should provide feedback to their teachers. The worst case is that a class – perhaps even with the help of an unknown technical solution – is suddenly asked to give teacher feedback without prior information: "So, now give me some feedback!" This cannot work.

Consequences of feedback

Feedback must provide a recognizable benefit for students. This is shown by the fact that critical feedback in certain areas also leads to perceivable changes. If this is not the case, the feedback practice will inevitably get stuck. Students cannot understand why they should provide feedback if nothing changes.

Keeping the time expenditure low

It is also important to keep the time required for gathering and processing feedback as short as possible. Digital solutions such as www.visiblefeedback.com can be helpful for this. However, technical solutions do not replace implementation. They merely make it easier.

Correctly used – also in view of the limited time resources of teachers – student feedback is used to talk about teaching. This way it is possible to create a real feedback culture in schools. The following checklist may help to consider the most important requirements for a successful feedback culture.

Checklist

- The teaching staff was properly informed on the subject.
- There are opportunities for the entire teaching staff to reflect on their own mindframe towards student feedback.
- A clear distinction between student feedback, teacher evaluation, and professional assessment (especially by the school board) is guaranteed.
- Student feedback is anchored in the school profile.
- Teachers can try out student feedback and receive support if necessary.
- School committees such as the staff council, parents' council, and school forum have agreed to the introduction of student feedback.
- The benefits have been made clear to all those involved (teachers, students, and parents).
- It has been explicitly pointed out that student feedback always must be discussed together with the feedback providers in a debriefing session.
- Any technical solutions used have been approved by the school's data privacy officer.

Feedback as part of professionalism

- What does pedagogical professionalism mean to you?
- What distinguishes teachers from other professionals? When do you think a doctor, lawyer, or psychologist acts in a professional way?

Professional basketball player Michael Jordan sums up his career in this way:

> I've missed more than 9,000 shots in my career. I've lost almost 300 games. 26 times, I've been trusted to take the game winning shot and missed. I've failed over and over and over again in my life. And that is why I succeed.
>
> (Etnier, 2009, p. 87)

Jordan summarizes his attitude by saying that he is ready to learn from mistakes and to work hard every day to become better. Does this also apply to you as a teacher?

There are many different opinions about what professionalism means in the school sector. One central point, however, is common to almost all types of definition of professionalism: the willingness to reflect upon one's own actions. Reflectivity is a core area of professionalism. This is illustrated not least by the way in which teachers succeed in justifying their work to learners, to themselves, to colleagues, to parents, and to the public. If teachers do not have an answer to the question of why they do what they do in class, then it is a sign they are lacking professionalism (cf. Paseka et al., 2011, p. 28, and Reh, 2004).

If professionalism is understood as critical self-reflection, then the question arises: How does it manifests itself – by thinking about what was going on in the classroom on your own? Or by searching for objective evidence of what went well and what did not go so well in class? Since the first option often points in the wrong direction, it is the second that has to be focused on. Without feedback, without talking about learning and teaching, reflection cannot be effective. Student feedback is essential in this respect and forms the core of the "evidence-based practitioner" (a term used by John Hattie in his presentations).

Evidence-based practitioners

Evidence-based practitioners test the effectiveness and fit of existing routines on the basis of empirically acquired criteria. They form routines in their profession, but not without constantly questioning them with regard to external data.

Student feedback in teacher training

Teacher trainees are the only teachers who receive relatively frequent feedback about their teaching – in the form of lesson visitations by teacher trainers and graded lessons. However, they receive this feedback exclusively from the persons who instruct and at the same time evaluate them.

But can feedback that is relevant for your future career lead you to reflect more on your work, thus furthering your professionalization, or does the existing practice perhaps even counteract this, since many new entrants to the profession are happy to no longer receive feedback after they have completed their training? A hierarchical gradient in the feedback situation and the blurred boundary between feedback and evaluation can lead to negative emotions towards feedback from the outset. Of course, one can ask oneself why even more feedback should play a central role in teacher training.

What feedback would you, as a job starter, like to get? A "should have, could have, might have" conversation, as described in Chapter 4, or an analysis of your lesson based on scientifically proven criteria of teaching quality to which you can compare different perspectives? Which of these conversations would you consider more profitable as a teacher trainer?

Conventional discussions about teaching often focus on whether there have been enough methodological variations, whether the introduction was original, or whether enough time was used for self-regulated learning – things that Hattie describes as the surface features of teaching. In so doing, these discussions completely ignore whether achievement has actually been enhanced. It is precisely on this criterion that teachers often lack information, although it would be very easy to obtain: Students could provide it. In addition, there is often a lack of real evidence, and the indications provided are based primarily on subjective everyday theories.

Missing, rare, or exclusively evaluative feedback is an important risk factor for low self-efficacy experience, and as a consequence for health problems, especially for young professionals. Isn't it at least plausible that both the acceptance and effectiveness of feedback procedures could be increased by the fact that they are exemplified by teacher trainers as role models?

Even for those traditional training methods that prove to be ineffective, there are alternatives that deal directly with feedback. An important example is microteaching, in which the behavior of teachers is filmed in very clearly defined teaching situations and then gradually changed. The effect size for microteaching in Visible Learning is 0.88! Why is this procedure rarely used in practice, although it has proven to be highly effective? Is this not particularly astonishing, since the lack of application transfer of what is learned during training is a major problem of teacher training (cf. Wahl, 2013; Wisniewski, 2016)?

What rational reason is there for the fact that student feedback still encounters great resistance from teacher trainers and trainees? The large number of excellent instruments that now exist for this purpose opens up great opportunities (not only) for young teachers.

No matter whether you are at the beginning of your professional career as a trainee, whether you are an experienced teacher, or whether you are a teacher trainer – ask yourself the following questions: What is important to you in your lessons? What indications you have that this is also important to your students?

How can you justify what you do?

Competence and mindframes as guarantors of success

It is one of the most persistent myths in educational science that a successful teacher is one who possesses a particularly high level of expertise in his or her subjects. The whole of university teacher training is based on this assumption and accordingly gives the greatest importance to subject matter knowledge. Whenever reforms in teacher training are discussed, the call for more subject matter knowledge has a firm place (Baumert & Kunter, 2006; Blömeke et al., 2010; Kunter et al, 2011; Pant et al., 2013). Assuming that teaching is an interaction between students and the teacher, who meet in the subject matter, an explanation is quickly found (cf. Zierer, 2015):

We have all met people who have a tremendous amount of knowledge but cannot explain it to others. They lack didactic competence. And we all know people who know an enormous amount of things, but are so inaccessible and cannot relate to their counterparts. They lack pedagogical competence. In this respect, professional competence alone is not enough to teach successfully. It must be accompanied by didactic and pedagogical competence – and only in this triad can it become effective. The call for more subject matter knowledge is therefore void – which does not mean that it is unnecessary. But we don't need more knowledge, we need teaching that brings the already existing level of knowledge to life. Didactic and pedagogical competence are decisive for this.

Figure 6.3 is an attempt to illustrate what has been said (cf. Zierer, 2015; Hattie & Zierer, 2017).

Research confirms this conclusion, if you read the existing studies correctly: For example, the IQB international comparison (see Pant et al., 2013) examined whether teachers who have studied a subject were more successful in teaching than teachers who did not. Indeed, the results show that this is the case. But to conclude from this that this result can be attributed solely to greater subject matter knowledge is not enough. Teachers who have studied one subject gained an increase in their didactic and pedagogical competence, especially during their practical training.

As convincing as these considerations may be, even the triad of subject matter knowledge, didactic competence, and pedagogical

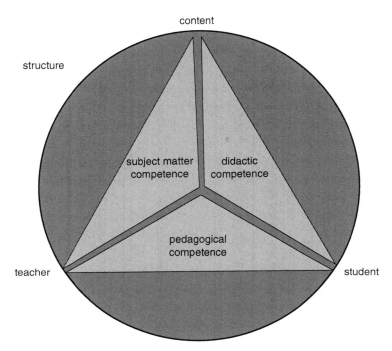

FIGURE 6.3 Competencies in the didactic triangle

competence is not enough to teach successfully. Rather, it is not so much what we do that matters, but also – and above all – how and why we do something. In this respect, it is not competence in the form of knowledge and ability that is decisive, but rather mindframes in the form of will and judgment. Figure 6.4 is another attempt to illustrate this idea (cf. Zierer, 2015, and Hattie & Zierer, 2017).

Against this backdrop, and in order to further clarify the ideas employed, it is worth taking a look at the results of expert research, such as those provided by Howard Gardner, Mihly Csikszentmihalyi, and William Damon in their Good Work Project (see Gardner et al., 2002). Professional success is based on three Es: excellence, engagement, and ethics. The core hypothesis is that only when all three aspects are recognizable and present can people succeed in their profession. Successful teaching is not only a question of knowledge and ability but also of will and judgment. In addition to competence (in the subject, in pedagogy, and in didactics) one's mindframe also plays a role. In fact, it ultimately even decides whether or not the knowledge and ability can be used. Interestingly, there is a clear connection between these aspects: Ability is based on knowledge but can be displayed only when there is a will to do so – and there are always reasons for this, so that will is based on judgment. Pedagogical action is deeply ethical. For example, if a teacher has access to the necessary knowledge, ability, will, and judgment, he or she will act accordingly in a certain situation and, if the context is favorable, will be successful. If one of the four aspects is missing, the teacher will most likely fail. Figure 6.5 summarizes what has been said (cf. Zierer, 2015; Hattie & Zierer, 2017).

Successful teachers have a passion not only for the subject but also for didactics and pedagogy, students, and their profession. To become a successful teacher, this passion is necessary but not sufficient: It is also important to practice this challenging profession for a lifetime to *remain* a successful teacher.

If these considerations are transferred to successful feedback, one can conclude that obtaining successful feedback does not only require competence but also and above all mindframes. Uncertainty often arises at this point: Can mindframes be changed at all? Or is this something that is very important but can't be influenced? To answer this question, look back at your own life: Sometimes a drastic experience is enough to

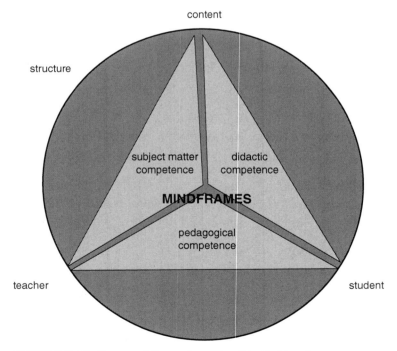

FIGURE 6.4 Mindframes at the center of the didactic triangle

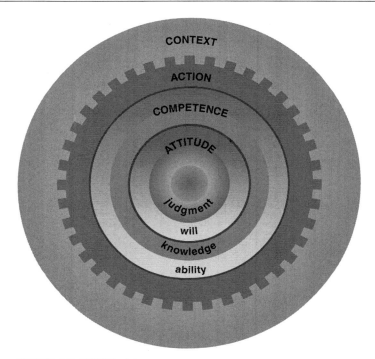

FIGURE 6.5 K3W Model

Source: Zierer (2015).

fundamentally change your own mindframes. Sometimes a great deal of effort proves to be ineffective. This makes it obvious: Working on mindframes is not easy. While competencies can be acquired in five minutes, work on mindframes undoubtedly requires more time, more courage, more stamina, and more effort. But should we therefore shy away from this and not take this important step in professionalization? Quite the contrary: If mindframes are so important, then it is precisely the hallmark of professionalism to meet this challenge. Generally speaking, there are two approaches to starting work on mindframes: first, through an expansion of competence that leads to new experiences and in turn has a lasting effect on mindframes; and second, through disclosure and analysis of existing mindframes. It is best if both approaches work together.

Make sure to check your feedback! Come to talk about it and exchange ideas! To do so, use Questionnaire 5 again, work on it alone, and discuss the different opinions with your colleagues.

The successful implementation of feedback will depend on giving teachers reasons why they should take the step. In this respect, it will be necessary to impart competencies and initiate mindframes.

The following appeal forms the conclusion, which tries to get to the heart of what has been mentioned in this book (cf. Hattie & Zierer, 2017):

- Providing feedback is different from receiving feedback: Watch out for the language used by students, parents, and colleagues!
- Feedback requires a positive understanding of errors: Errors are welcome!
- Feedback points out weaknesses: Set the challenge! Learning means hard work!
- Feedback requires a positive atmosphere: Working on relationships is important!
- Feedback is not a one-way street: Use all data about your teaching! Use all feedback levels!
- Know your impact in a democratic school!

Bibliography

Baumert, J., & Kunter, M. (2006). Stichwort: Professionelle Kompetenz von Lehrkräften. *Zeitschrift für Erziehungswissenschaft*, 9(4), 469–520.

Blömeke, S., Kaiser, G., & Lehmann, R. (Hrsg.). (2010). *TEDS-M 2008. Professionelle Kompetenz und Lerngelegenheiten angehender Primarstufenlehrkräfte im internationalen Vergleich*. Münster: Waxmann.

Endres, A., & Martiensen, J. (2007). *Mikroökonomik: Eine integrierte Darstellung traditioneller und moderner Konzepte in Theorie und Praxis*. Stuttgart: Kohlhammer.

Enns, E., Rüegg, R., Schindler, B., & Strahm, P. (2004). *Lehren und Lernen im Tandem. Porträt eines partnerschaftlichen Fortbildungssystems*. Bern: Zentralstelle für Lehrerinnen-und Lehrerfortbildung.

Etnier, J. L. (2009). *Bring your A game: A young athlete's guide to mental toughness*. Chapel Hill: University of North Carolina Press.

Gardner, H., Csikszentmihalyi, M., & Damon, W. (2002). *Good work: When excellence and ethics meet*. New York: Basic Books.

Hattie, J. (2008). *Visible Learning: A synthesis of over 800 meta-analyses relating to achievement*. London: Routledge.

Hattie, J., & Zierer, K. (2017). *10 mindframes for visible learning: Teaching for success*. London: Routledge.

Kunter, M., Baumert, J., & Blum, W. (Hrsg.). (2011). *Professionelle Kompetenz von Lehrkräften: Ergebnisse des Forschungsprogramms COACTIV*. Münster: Waxmann.

Pant, H. A., Stanat, P., Schroeders, U., Roppelt, A., Siegle, T., & Pöhlmann, C. (2013). *IQB-Ländervergleich 2012: Mathematische und naturwissenschaftliche Kompetenzen am Ende der Sekundarstufe I*. Münster: Waxmann.

Paseka, I., Schraz, M., &Schrittesser, I. (2011). Professionstheoretische Grundlagen und thematische Annäherung. In Ebd. (Hrsg.), *Pädagogische Professionalität quer denken – umdenken- neu denken*. Wien: Facultas, S. 187–217.

Reh, S. (2004). Abschied von der Profession, von Professionalität oder vom Professionellen? Theorien und Forschungen zur Lehrerprofessionalität. *Zeitschrift für Pädagogik*, 50(3), 358–372.

Rogers, E. (1995). *The diffusion of innovations*, New York: Free Press.

Roth, S. (2000). Emotionen im Visier: Neue Wege des Change Managements. *OrganisationsEntwicklung*, 2/2000, 14–21.

Terhart, E. (2002). Wie können die Ergebnisse von vergleichenden Leistungsstudien systematisch zur Qualitätsverbesserung in Schulen genutzt werden? *Zeitschrift für Pädagogik*, 48(1), 91–110.

Wahl, D. (2013). *Lernumgebungen erfolgreich gestalten*. Bad Heilbrunn: Klinkhardt.

Wisniewski, B. (2016). Vom fundierten Wissen zur reflektierten Praxis – Möglichkeiten und Grenzen der Professionalisierung in der Lehrerbildung. *Schulmagazin 5–10*, 11/2016, 11–14.

Zierer, K. (2015). Educational expertise: The concept of "mind frames" as an integrative model for professionalisation in teaching. *Oxford Review of Education*, 41(6), 782–798.

Index

7Cs 57–59; *see also* quality of teaching

academic achievement 8; *see also* student achievement
acquiescence 55
ad-hoc feedback *see* questionnaire
assessment 24, 27, 31, 32–33

behavioral change 54, 63, 66, 72–75
blind spot *see Johari window*

captivate *see* 7Cs
care *see* 7Cs
challenge *see* 7Cs
clarify *see* 7Cs
classroom climate 81–83
coaching 71–74
cognitive dissonance 68
collegial feedback 12
comparison of perspectives 81–82
confer *see* 7Cs
consolidate *see* 7Cs
control *see* 7Cs
counseling 62, 74
criticism 44, 68, 77
culture of errors 24–25

dangers of feedback 66–68
debriefing 61–62, 73–74, 92, 101
deficit orientation 96
development effect *see* effects of teaching
didactic competence 104–106
didactic hexagon 34
didactic triangle 105–106
digital solutions 31, 66, 77, 100
door opener 48–50

effect size 7–9
effects of teaching 7–9
emotion 68, 103
evaluation 27–28, 32–33
evidence-based practitioner 102
evidence-based questionnaires *see* questionnaire
evidence-based teaching 13
expert 18–19
extrinsic *see* motivation

feedback chart 47
feedback coordinate system 45
feedback culture 95–98
feedback matrix 20
feedback methods 49
feedback mindframes 100
feedback provider 20–24
feedback recipient 20–24
feedback target 46
feed-forward *see* perspectives of feedback
feed-up *see* perspectives of feedback
functional attachment 69

Gates Foundation 52–53, 56
grading: of students 41–44; of teachers 32–34, 68

implementation *see* innovation
in-depth understanding *see task type*
innovation 96–101
instructional quality *see* quality of teaching
intrsinsic *see* motivation

job satisfaction 30, 96
Johari window 29–30

Index

K3W model 107

learner-learner feedback 22
levels of feedback 14–18

meta-analysis 7, 11
MET project 57, 59
microteaching 103
mindframe 95, 99–100, 104–107
motivation 14–15
myth 6, 31–32, 104

novice 18

objectivity 51
one-sentence flash repsonse 52

paedagogical competence 104–106
paper-pencil instruments 31, 66
personality *see* levels of feedback
perspectives of feeback 19–20
praise 14–15
process *see* levels of feedback
professional development 28, 65; *see also* professionalization
professionalization 104–107

quality of teaching 32, 52–53, 55, 58, 86
questionnaire 46–50, 52–56

reactance 69
reference standard 43
reliability 51
reorganization *see* task type

reproduction *see* task type
response distortion 51, 55
response distribution 81
reverse effect *see* effects of teaching

school attendance effect *see* effects of teaching
self *see* levels of feedback
self-awareness 66–67
self-concept 96; *see also* self-perception
self-efficacy 67, 69–70, 76
self-esteem 49, 54, 69
self-image 14, 32; *see also* self-perception
self-perception 32, 47, 69, 81, 94
self-reflection 65–68, 102
self-regulation *see* levels of feedback
self-serving bias 69
student achievement 8, 11
student-student relationships 83–85
SWOT analysis 70–71

target agreement 61
task *see* levels of feedback
task type 41–45
teaCh 56–60; *see also* questionnaire
teacher feedback 12
teacher health 30
teacher-student relationship 15, 84
teacher training 102–104
transfer *see* task type

validated *see* questionnaire
validity 51
value-added score 53